CW00695874

Sent Proclaim the Gospel

Honouring the legacy of St Paul VI

Jim McManus C.Ss.R.

redemptorist
publications

Published by **Redemptorist Publications**
Alphonsus House, Chawton, Hampshire, GU34 3HQ, UK
Tel. +44 (0)1420 88222, Fax +44 (0)1420 88805
Email rp@rpbooks.co.uk, www.rpbooks.co.uk

A registered charity limited by guarantee
Registered in England 3261721

Copyright © Redemptorist Publications 2018
First published October 2018

Text by Jim McManus C.Ss.R.
Edited by Katie Stockermans
Designed by Christine Towner
Cover Design by Emma Repetti

ISBN 978-0-85231-529-3

All rights reserved. No part of this publication may be reproduced, stored in a retrieval system, or transmitted in any form or by any means, electronic, mechanical, photocopying, recording or otherwise, without prior permission in writing from Redemptorist Publications.

The moral right of the author to be identified as the author of this work has been asserted in accordance with the Copyright, Designs and Patents Act 1988.

A CIP catalogue record for this book is available from the British Library

The publisher gratefully acknowledges permission to use the following copyright material:

Excerpts from THE JERUSALEM BIBLE, copyright © 1974, 1989 by Darton, Longman & Todd, Ltd and Doubleday, a division of Random House, Inc. Reprinted by permission.

Excerpts from the New Revised Standard Version of the Bible: Anglisied Edition, © 1989, 1995, Division of Christian Education of the National Council of the Churches of Christ in the United States of America. Used by permission. All rights reserved.

Printed by 4edge Limited, Essex SS5 4AD

Other titles by Jim McManus C.Ss.R.
available from Redemptorist Publications
www.rpbooks.co.uk

The Healing Power of the Sacraments

Healing in the Spirit

Hallowed Be Thy Name

All Generations Will Call Me Blessed

The Inside Job: a spirituality of true self-esteem

I Am My Body: Blessed John Paul's theology of the body

Finding Forgiveness: personal and spiritual perspectives
(with Dr Stephanie Thornton)

Searching for Serenity: spirituality in later life
(with Dr Stephanie Thornton)

Going to Mass: becoming the Eucharist we celebrate

Fountain of Grace: celebrating 150 years of the Icon of Love

Embraced by Mercy: God's ultimate gift

At Home in the Mysteries of Christ: the grace of the Rosary

Our Spiritual Lifeline: the oxygen of Christian prayer

I dedicate this book to our Redemptorist Lay Associates who are full of enthusiasm for preaching the Good News of Jesus Christ.

— Contents —

— Foreword —

Ralph Heskett C.Ss.R.
Bishop of Hallam

The final words spoken to us by a loved one have a special significance for us. They are words that are rarely very far from recall and often play a significant role in forming us into the people we become. This is certainly true of the final words of Jesus to his disciples. All three synoptic Gospels record Jesus' final words to his disciples, each making specific reference to his commission to "Go… make disciples of all nations".

Christ's followers in every age are indeed truly privileged and blessed to be trusted with this great commission by the Lord on behalf of the world. From the time of the great missionary bishops of the Early Church down to the present day, disciples of Jesus have taken up this responsibility and challenge with enthusiasm. For some, the challenge came at some personal cost, even life itself. Each new generation of disciples is called to respond to this ancient commission in a new way – whatever the cost. It is an invitation and challenge, therefore, that is forever old and forever new.

Drawing on his own experience as a kerygmatic preacher and retreat director and on the teaching of the Church, especially the writings of St Paul VI, St John Paul II, Pope Emeritus Benedict XVI and Pope Francis, Fr McManus gives a very personal and practical reflection on the nature of our call to the ministry of evangelisation and how we might respond to this call as individuals and as parish communities.

We have to share good news with our friends. I still remember my compulsion to share the good news that I had passed my driving test on the third attempt. I was a student in our seminary at the time. The test took place just before Christmas. I couldn't believe my good fortune when the examiner uttered the words: "That concludes the test Mr Heskett and I am pleased to say that you have passed." I ran back to the college to share my good news with my brothers. Then I remembered that I had left a silent pre-Christmas retreat to take the test. What was I to do? Should I keep my good news until the retreat was over or break the silence of the retreat and share my good news there and then? I couldn't contain myself and did the latter. But that's the thing about good news – it has to be shared!

This strong desire and impulse to share our good news with others is at the heart of the ministry of evangelisation. In the work of evangelisation, of course, the good news is the story of God's wonderful deeds for his people. Not surprisingly, therefore, Fr McManus emphasises the importance of the proclamation of the kerygma, which is the fundamental Christian story. It can be summed up in the following six statements I recently came across: the love of God; the reality of sin; Jesus' death for sinners; the need for repentance and faith; the gift of the Holy Spirit; and becoming part of the Church.

More particularly, the ministry of evangelisation includes a word that expresses our own personal experience of what the Lord has done for us and continues to do for us – an opportunity to share something of our personal relationship with Jesus. And, of course, before ever we speak a word, we must live the life, showing by the manner of our life that we are disciples of Jesus. I am reminded of the words attributed to St Francis of Assisi: "Preach Jesus and, if necessary, use words." Only the person who knows Jesus through their personal encounter with him (and not simply knows about him) can truly evangelise. We need take only the most casual look at the Acts of the Apostles and the letters of St Paul. In his second letter to the church at Corinth, for example, he gives his reason for returning to his fundamental vision of what Christ did for us:

> For the love of Christ urges us on, because we are convinced that one has died for all; therefore all have died. And he died for all, so that those who live might live no longer for themselves, but for him who died and was raised for them.
>
> 2 Corinthians 5:14-15

We are not expected to – indeed we cannot – witness to the wonderful works of God in the world and in ourselves, if we are trying to work through our own strength. So, Jesus' great commission is accompanied by his assurance to his disciples then and now: "And remember, I am with you always, to the end of the age" (Matthew 28:20).

In the work of evangelisation, we are invited to participate with the Spirit who is its principle agent. The Spirit encourages and guides us individually to do three things: to proclaim the Gospel, to open our hearts to receive the word and to help us to discern the signs of the times. Indeed, to engage in the ministry of evangelisation without the gentle action of the Holy Spirit is a fruitless and powerless exercise. In *Evangelii Nuntiandi* ("Evangelization in the Modern World"), St Paul VI beautifully highlights this vital role of the Holy Spirit in the work of evangelisation in these words:

> Techniques of evangelization are good, but even the most advanced ones could not replace the gentle action of the Spirit. The most perfect preparation of the evangelizer has no effect without the Holy Spirit. Without the Holy Spirit the most convincing dialectic has no power over the heart of man. [1]

We live in a world today where many put forward the notion of a way of living as if God does not exist. The result is a world robbed

---

1   St Paul VI, *Evangelii Nuntiandi* ("Evangelization in the Modern World"), 75.

of hope. It is more urgent than ever, therefore, that we give witness to the hope that is in us.

In the preface to his book Fr McManus has this word for his readers:

> My hope in writing this book is that you will be filled with the joy of the Holy Spirit as you reflect on your own vocation as a missionary disciple in today's Church. You have good news for the world.

I think his book will do this and more.

— Preface —

Reflecting on preaching the Gospel is as old as Christianity itself. We were commissioned by the Lord to preach the good news of our salvation. Each new generation has to begin again, in its own culture, to proclaim that Jesus Christ is risen from the dead, that he is the saviour of the human race. Without that preaching people would never come to faith in Jesus Christ. St Paul said very clearly:

> But how are they to call on one in whom they have not believed? And how are they to believe in one whom they have never heard? And how they are to hear without someone to proclaim him? And how are they to proclaim him unless they are sent?
>
> Romans 10:14-15

Who are the preachers who are being sent today? St John Paul II said: "The commitment of the laity to the work of evangelization is changing ecclesial life,"[1] that is, the life of the Church. Clergy, of course, have always been seen as preachers of the Gospel but today, in our changing Church and world, the Holy Spirit is raising up new regiments of preachers, of evangelisers, from the ranks of the laity all over the Church. Each lay person in the Church of today is "a missionary disciple" sent by Christ to proclaim the good news of salvation. It is a spiritual mission and we have to reflect on it in a spiritual way, listening to what the Spirit is saying in our own hearts. The evangeliser is the one who must first be evangelised.

In the first chapter we will look at that immense mission that Jesus gave to his Twelve Apostles, to go into the whole world and the proclaim the Gospel. We will see, how in God's plan for the

---

1   St John Paul II, *Redemptoris Missio* ("Mission of the Redeemer"), 2.

evangelisation of our world, the Holy Spirit is inspiring laymen and laywomen to live a fulfilled Christian life by sharing their faith with others. Pope Francis, in his groundbreaking document *Evangelii Gaudium* ("The Joy of the Gospel") expresses this well and with a sense of humour:

> When the Church summons Christians to take up the task of evangelization, she is simply pointing to the source of authentic personal fulfilment. For "here we discover a profound law of reality: that life is attained and matures in the measure that it is offered up in order to give life to others. This is certainly what mission means". Consequently, an evangelizer must never look like someone who has just come from a funeral! Let us recover and deepen our enthusiasm, that "delightful and comforting joy of evangelizing, even when it is in tears that we must sow…"[2]

In the second chapter we will reflect on the deepest identity of the Church. In the words of St Paul VI we have to say:

> Evangelizing is in fact the grace and vocation proper to the Church, her deepest identity. She exists to evangelize…[3]

The Church is not there simply for Catholics or other Christians. She is there for the whole human race.

In the third chapter we will ask ourselves where we get the motivation to become evangelisers. It flows from our own identity as disciples of Jesus Christ, commissioned by him to make him known to others. In the words of St John Paul II:

> The burning desire to invite others to encounter the One whom we have encountered is the start of the evangelizing mission to which the whole Church is called.[4]

---

2   *Evangelii Gaudium*, 10.
3   St Paul VI, *Evangelii Nuntiandi* ("Evangelisation in the Modern World"), 14.
4   St John Paul II, *Ecclesia in America* ("The Church in America"), 68.

Our fourth chapter reflects on how we prepare our minds and hearts for the work of evangelisation. We will be looking again at the work of the Spirit in our lives and at our own life of prayer. If we want to make Christ known to others we have to get to know him more intimately each day.

The fifth chapter reflects on how parishioners can best prepare their parish for the work of evangelisation. It has to be or become an "oasis of mercy", where all are made welcome and feel accepted, loved, esteemed and valued. Each missionary disciple in the parish has to be prepared to undergo a daily conversion so that they can love others as Christ loves them.

The sixth chapter is devoted to the message that Christ asks us to proclaim, namely, the good news of his death and resurrection for the salvation of the world. This is the primary proclamation of the Gospel. We use an ancient Greek word for it and call it the kerygma. It is about what Christ has done for each person.

Finally, in the seventh chapter we will reflect on how we proclaim the death and the resurrection of Jesus Christ as a community when we gather to celebrate the Mass. As St Paul said: "For as often as you eat this bread and drink the cup, you proclaim the Lord's death until he comes." (1 Corinthians 11:26)

My hope in writing this book is that you will be filled with the joy of the Holy Spirit as you reflect on your own vocation as a missionary disciple in today's Church. You have good news for the world.

At the end of each chapter I will invite you to enter into the stillness of your own heart and be still with the God of mercy who makes his home in you. This will be a moment for interiorising the main message of each chapter. It will help you to get the message out of your head and into your heart. Each day you will be blessed if you can find some time to enter into this stillness in God's presence.

My sincere thanks to Bishop Ralph Heskett C.Ss.R. for writing the foreword to this book. Bishop Ralph has been a great preacher of the Gospel throughout his life

My thanks also to Marie Hogg, a Redemptorist Lay Associate. She gives parish missions and courses in spirituality with me and co-directs our seven-week sabbatical courses at our Renewal Centre in Perth. She read the manuscript carefully and made very helpful suggestions.

I am most grateful also to the staff and editors at Redemptorist Publications for publishing this book.

— Chapter 1 —

Mission to the whole world

Just before Jesus ascended into heaven he gave this amazing commission to his disciples with these words:

> All authority in heaven and on earth has been given to me. Go therefore and make disciples of all nations, baptising them in the name of the Father and of the Son and of the Holy Spirit, and teaching them to obey everything that I have commanded you. And remember, I am with you always, to the end of the age.
>
> Matthew 28:18-20

Those first disciples, few in number and with little formal education, set out at the Lord's command to fulfil their mission. They travelled all over the ancient pagan Roman Empire announcing extraordinary news, namely, that Jesus Christ, who had been crucified by the Roman governor in Jerusalem, had risen from the dead. This same Jesus had sent the Holy Spirit upon them, and commanded them to go in the power of the Spirit and make disciples of all nations. Some people must have thought that they were completely out of their minds. The gods and goddesses of the Roman Empire were powerful and jealous. Jupiter, the king of the gods and goddesses, or Mars the god of war, would scorn any attempt to dethrone them and put Jesus Christ in their place. Yet, within twenty to thirty years after the death and resurrection of Jesus, St Paul was writing to Churches founded in great cities like Thessalonica and Corinth in Greece, Ephesus in Turkey, and Rome itself, the centre of the pagan Roman Empire, thousands of miles away from Jerusalem, encouraging and instructing Christians who had accepted Jesus Christ as their risen Lord and Saviour. Indeed, in his letter to the Colossians, St Paul wrote:

> The Good News which has reached you is spreading all over the world and producing the same results as it has among you ever since the day when you heard about God's grace and understood what this really is.
>
> Colossians 1:5-6

Just within a few decades after the crucifixion of Jesus Christ, St Paul was telling people that the good news was spreading all over the world. Those first disciples were doing what Jesus sent them forth to do, namely, "to proclaim the good news" that Jesus is risen from the dead, that he is the Saviour of the human race, that he forgives all sin and renews in the Holy Spirit all who accept him as their Lord and Saviour and gives them eternal life. St Paul spelt out this amazing message to the Romans with these words:

> If the Spirit of him who raised Jesus from the dead dwells in you, he who raised Jesus Christ from the dead will give life to your mortal bodies also through his Spirit that dwells in you.
>
> Romans 8:11

That was truly great and exciting news for men and women who lived without hope and in fear of death.

The apostles, who were the first to proclaim that Jesus Christ is risen from the dead, were so successful in proclaiming the Gospel of Jesus that the only way the Roman Empire could deal with them was to kill them. They died the death of martyrs. The Gospel which Jesus Christ had entrusted to them and commissioned them to proclaim to the whole world meant far more to them than living a few more years as fishermen around the lake of Galilee. Only one thing was important in their lives and that was to proclaim throughout the world the death and resurrection of Jesus Christ for the salvation of humanity.

Throughout the long history of the Church the disciples of Christ have continued to do the great work of evangelisation, proclaiming

Jesus Christ as the Saviour of the whole human race. Many of them met the same violent death as the apostles. Through their very martyrdom they became the great witnesses to the risen Lord Jesus Christ. Even today, in the twenty-first century, thousands of Christians, of all the denominations, have been martyred because they refused to give up their faith in Christ. Pope Francis spoke of this great witness when he welcomed His Holiness Karekin II, supreme patriarch of the Armenian Church to the Vatican in 2014:

> Your Holiness, dear Brothers, the sufferings endured by Christians in these last decades have made a unique and invaluable contribution to the unity of Christ's disciples. As in the ancient Church, the blood of the martyrs became the seed of new Christians. So too in our time the blood of innumerable Christians has become a seed of unity. The ecumenism of suffering and of the martyrdom of blood are a powerful summons to walk the long path of reconciliation between the Churches, by courageously and decisively abandoning ourselves to the working of the Holy Spirit.[5]

Fr Cantalamessa identified four great waves of evangelisation in the history of the Church.[6] We will take just a glimpse at this extraordinary history.

Missionary bishops during the second, third, fourth and fifth centuries

The first great wave of evangelisation in the early centuries of the Church, in the ancient Roman empire, was led by missionary bishops, great saints and many of them martyrs, like St Ignatius of Antioch, St Polycarp of Smyrna, St Irenaeus of Lyons, and St Patrick who evangelised Ireland. They built on the foundation laid by the apostles and the missionary disciples of the first and second centuries.

---

5   Pope Francis, 8 May 2014 (Zenit.org).
6   Fr Cantalamessa, 12 May 2014 (Zenit.org).

Missionary monks of the fifth to ninth centuries

With the emergence of the monastic movement in the fifth century we had a second wave of evangelisation. The monks played a key role in re-evangelising Europe in these centuries. Their monasteries became houses of prayer, evangelisation and education. The Roman Empire had collapsed under the constant pressure of the barbarian invasions. These were Germanic tribes, the Huns, Goths and Vandals, migrating west in search of better homelands. The missionary monks had to begin the evangelisation of these new inhabitants of Europe. The Benedictine movement spread from Italy throughout Europe. The Church in Ireland in those early centuries was very monastic. Great missionary monks like St Columba, who founded his monastery on the island of Iona, evangelised throughout Scotland; St Aidan came from Iona to Lindisfarne and became known as the apostle of Northumbria. He and his monks preached the Gospel all over the north of England. St Augustine of Canterbury came from Rome to preach the Gospel to the Germanic tribes, the Anglo Saxons, who had emigrated from the continent and established their kingdom in Kent. St David founded monastic communities in Wales and preached the Gospel throughout Wales. St Boniface preached the Gospel in Germany. St Columbanus and St Killian, and St Brendan, with their communities, evangelised all over Europe in the sixth, seventh and eighth centuries. Those great missionary monks had the support of the prayers of those who never left their monasteries. Evangelisation is always the fruit of prayer and preaching.

Friars and the new religious orders and the evangelisation of the New World[7]

In the sixteenth century the third wave of evangelisation began. European explorers, men like Christopher Columbus and Vasco de Gama had reached the Americas, both north and south and had sailed to India, China and Japan. European nations, England, Spain and

---

7 I can name just a few of the hundreds of religious orders and congregations who made such wonderful and dynamic contributions in the third great wave of evangelisation.

Portugal, began to colonise the Americas. The indigenous people in this new world had never heard of Christ. They were in need of evangelisation. The new evangelisers were the friars of the different orders of Franciscans, the Dominicans, Carmelites, and the Jesuits, an order which had been founded in 1534 by St Ignatius Loyola.

In the seventeenth, eighteenth, nineteenth and twentieth centuries new religious congregations of men were founded for the missions: the Congregation of the Missions (Vincentians), founded by St Vincent de Paul in 1624; the Holy Ghost Fathers, now known as the Spiritans, founded by Claude Poullart des Places in 1703; the Passionists, founded by St Paul of the Cross in 1725; the Redemptorists, founded by St Alphonsus de Liguori in1732; the Salesian Fathers, founded by St John Bosco in 1845; the Society of African Missions (S.M.A. Fathers), founded by Melchior de Marion Bresillac in 1856; the Mill Hill Fathers, founded by the Archbishop of Westminster, Cardinal Vaughan, in 1866; the Columban Fathers, founded by Bishop Edward Galvin in 1916; the Kiltegan Fathers, founded in 1932 by Monsignor Patrick Whitney. There were many other congregations of missionary priests founded throughout the Catholic Church in the past four hundred years for the work of the missions.

Congregations of religious sisters

The Church was greatly enriched and the work of evangelisation immensely enhanced by the great numbers of active, missionary congregations of women who evangelised through their commitment to education, medical care, care for the sick, the elderly and orphans. Founded by visionary and holy women to witness to Christ by their work, they made Christ known to millions. I will mention only a few: the Daughters of Charity, founded by St Vincent de Paul and St Louise de Marillac in 1633; the Presentation Sisters, founded by Nano Nagle in 1775; the Sisters of Mercy, founded by the Venerable Catherine McAuley in 1831; the Little Sisters of the Poor, founded by St Jeanne Jugan in 1839; the Salesian Sisters of St John Bosco, founded by St Maria Mazzerello in 1872; the Medical Missionaries of Mary, founded by Mother Mary Martin in 1937; the Missionaries of Charity, founded by Mother Theresa (St Theresa of Calcutta) in 1950.

Congregations of religious brothers
A large number of congregations of religious brothers were founded to witness to Christ through their schools and hospitals: the de La Salle Brothers, founded by St John Baptise de La Salle in 1679; the Patrician Brothers, founded by Bishop Delany in 1808; the Irish Christian Brothers, founded by Blessed Edmund Rice in 1808; the Presentation Brothers, who recognise Blessed Edmund Rice as their founder, were established in 1887. And a great many other congregations of brothers were founded all over the Church by saintly men who heard the call of Christ to go and "make disciples".

All these orders and congregations of men and women were the missionaries who evangelised the Americas, Africa and the Far East. The lay Catholics all over the Church supported these great missionaries with their money. Catholic parents willingly allowed their sons and daughters to join these orders and congregations and be sent off on the missions, even though that often meant leaving home never to return. The Church of our time, in every part of the world, owes a great debt of gratitude to these great men and women of the missions in the past four hundred years.

It is our turn now
Who will surf on the fourth great wave of evangelisation that is so urgently needed today and that has already begun? We are all aware that the number of religious priests, sisters and brothers has dramatically declined in Europe, the USA, Canada, Australia and New Zealand in the past fifty years. But God has been preparing a new army of evangelisers, men and women of all ages and of all nationalities, the lay faithful of the Church. Pope Francis identified this great army of Christ when he said:

All the baptized, whatever their position in the Church or their level of instruction in the faith, are agents of evangelization, and it would be insufficient to envisage a plan of evangelization to be carried out by professionals while the rest of the faithful would simply be passive recipients. The new evangelisation calls for personal involvement on the part of each of the baptized... we no longer say that we are "disciples" and "missionaries", but rather that we are always "missionary disciples".[8]

Missionary disciples

Pope Francis gives us this new identity: each of us is a missionary disciple. I will use his term throughout this book when I am referring to how we are involved in the mission of evangelisation. We are familiar with the word "disciples" but what does it really mean? It comes from a Greek word that means "a learner". Each one of us, as members of our parish community, can let the light of our own faith shine. If this light is not shining, the parish will never attract people who are searching for a deeper meaning in their life. As Pope Francis said: "It is not by proselytizing that the Church grows, but 'by attraction'".[9] You don't have to be a theologian or a teacher or a skilled communicator to let your light shine. But you have to be a disciple, one who is learning from the master, from Jesus. We do not settle for anything less than knowledge of our Lord Jesus Christ. He makes it very clear how we let the light of the Gospel shine. It is not through our intelligence, through our inventive skills in communication, but through our love for one another. He says: "By this everyone will know that you are my disciples, if you have love for one another" (John 13:35).

See how these Christians love one another

In our society, where people are not united by cultural or racial or sometimes even family ties, the warmth, hospitality and unity of

---

8   *Evangelii Gaudium*, 120.
9   Fr Cantalamessa, 12 May 2014 (Zenit.org).

the Catholic parish community makes a deep impression. The great early Christian convert, Tertullian, a famous lawyer, imagined the pagans in Rome saying to one another: "See how these Christians love one another." It was through their love for one another that those early Christians attracted people, often at great risk of persecution, to join their community. It was that love for one another, the gift of the Holy Spirit, that so shone the light of faith into people's lives that they wanted to share in that love. It gave meaning and purpose to their lives. They wanted to know the secret of how people of so many different backgrounds could love one another and form a warm, welcoming community. They were attracted by the love of the community and they discovered the secret of that love. They discovered that God is love and that Jesus Christ came among us to reveal God's love and has made it possible for us to share in it.

People today have a deep longing and yearning to be welcomed into a loving community. Loneliness is the plague of our age. Many millions of people in the Western world now describe themselves as chronically lonely, feeling lonely much or all of the time. For example, psychologist Dr Stephanie Thorton says that according to surveys in the UK in 2017, nine million people (nearly 14% of the population) described themselves as chronically lonely. The problem is most frequent in older people, where the percentage of the lonely is very much higher, but is growing more common in younger generations too. Similar or even worse results are reported in surveys from other Western societies: between 12% and 25% of French people describe themselves as lonely; over 40% of older Americans and around 60% of Australians say that they are lonely most of the time. These are shocking figures.

We long for community, to be part of something where we belong, where we matter. But many don't know how to find that refuge. In 2018 the British government appointed a minister with responsibility for reducing loneliness. This was an important step, acknowledging the importance and urgency of this issue. But whilst raising awareness of the problem is useful, it is effective action that will make the difference. In the past the Churches played a very decisive role to establishing communities. Wherever you go in Britain or Ireland you will see at the centre of every small town or village a church, or maybe several churches. In the big towns and cities you will see magnificent cathedrals and churches. These were places of community worship and fellowship where people had a sense of belonging.

Your parish could provide that sense of belonging to all who attend your church and attract many new members. Just imagine the light that would shine if you and a group of others decided that the hallmark of your parish life would be your love for one another. No exceptions, no exclusions, no cliques, no back biting, no slandering, just loving one another as Christ has loved you all. What a difference that would make! Your parish would truly be "an oasis of mercy" where the weary traveller who has lost his or her way in the desert of our big, impersonal cities, would find rest. As Pope Francis said:

> …wherever the Church is present, the mercy of the Father must be evident. In our parishes, communities, associations and movements, in a word, wherever there are Christians, everyone should find the oasis of mercy.[10]

A parish community that is "an oasis of mercy" is alive with love and ready to welcome all comers. This parish gives a powerful witness which people never fail to notice. They want to know the secret that keeps all these diverse people bonded together, happy in each other's company, joyfully meeting together every Sunday in their churches to pray, sing and celebrate. St Paul revealed their secret with these words: "This mystery… is Christ in you, the hope of glory" (Colossians 1:27). That love, unity and joy of a truly Christian community which attracts the attention, admiration and longing of a lonely outside observer is really a glimpse of the

---

10 Pope Francis, *Misericordiae Vultus* ("Bull of Indiction of the Extraodinary Jubilee of Mercy"), 12.

presence of Christ in the midst of the community. That community is witnessing to Christ. Pope Benedict XVI described what it means to witness with these words:

> We become witnesses when, through our actions, words and way of being, Another makes himself present.[11]

It is Christ himself whom people meet when they enter a truly loving community.

Be merciful, just as your Father is merciful

Disciples, as we have seen, are learners. We learn from Jesus how to live. When he says to us "Be merciful, just as your Father is merciful" (Luke 6:36) we seek to put his teaching into practice. Being merciful like our Father is the compelling reason for sharing our faith with others, for being the "missionary disciples" that Pope Francis calls each of us to be. We seek to make both a personal and a community response. On a personal level we relate to everyone in a truly respectful and loving way, seeing Christ in each other. We share our faith with whoever expresses any kind of interest. St Peter spoke about this when he said:

> In your hearts sanctify Christ as Lord. Always be ready to make your defence to anyone who demands from you an account for the hope that is in you; yet do it with gentleness and reverence. Keep your conscience clear, so that, when you are maligned, those who abuse you for your good conduct in Christ may be put to shame.
>
> 1 Peter 3:15-16

It is that gentleness and reverence which invites people to ask about our faith. Most people who join the Church say that it was the example of an individual that first attracted them to consider becoming a Catholic.

---

11 Pope Benedict XVI, *Sacramentum Caritatis* ("The Sacrament of Charity"), 85.

Dialogue

We may be sadly aware that our own parish never seems to attract the attention of the people in our area. Yet we believe that Jesus says to the people of our parish:

> You are the light of the world. A city built on a hill cannot be hid... In the same way, let your light shine before others, so that they may see your good works and give glory to your Father in heaven.
>
> Matthew 5:14-16

Your parish community is that city built on a hill. If the light is not yet shining brightly, the community should not just complain or shrug their shoulders or blame a few people. They could meet in prayer, invoking the Holy Spirit to come upon them as he came on the first disciples on that first Pentecost Day. They could pray: "Send forth your Spirit, O Lord, and renew the face of the earth". Over fifty years ago the Second Vatican Council was encouraging the parish community to meet, discuss and solve problems together. It stated:

> The laity should develop the habit of working in the parish in close cooperation with their priests, of bringing before the ecclesial community their own problems, world problems, and questions regarding humanity's salvation, to examine them together and solve them by general discussion. According to their abilities the laity ought to cooperate in all the apostolic and missionary enterprises of their ecclesial family.[12]

When the parish seeks to solve problems together, through sincere dialogue, the Holy Spirit is present and will lead the community to a good solution.

The joyful, warm and welcoming parish community is the Church's greatest asset for evangelisation. Your contribution to creating that

---

12   Second Vatican Council, *Apostolicam Actuositatem* (Decree on the Apostolate of Lay People), 10.

kind of community in your parish is indispensable. As you faithfully enter into the life of your parish community you become a witness to Christ, not just to the members of the parish, but through the joyful community that you help to create, to those all around your parish. That is why St John Paul II was inspired to write:

> God is opening before the Church the horizons of a humanity more fully prepared for the sowing of the Gospel. I sense that the moment has come to commit all of the Church's energies to a new evangelization...[13]

St John Paul II wanted to commit all the Church's energies to the new evangelisation. You could dialogue with your parish in a community meeting by asking what energies has the parish committed to this great mission of attracting others to Christ? Is your parish excited about getting involved in this new evangelisation? St John Paul II challenges each Christian community with these strong words:

> No Christian community is faithful to its duty unless it is missionary: either it is a *missionary community* or it is not even a *Christian community*...[14]

That is the great challenge to our parish communities today. Are we ready to face this challenge? Are we willing to be as merciful as our heavenly Father and bring the good news of his salvation to others? What would an evangelising parish look like? Pope Francis gives us a clear picture:

> An evangelizing community knows that the Lord has taken the initiative, he has loved us first (cf. 1 John 4:19), and therefore we can move forward, boldly take the initiative, go out to others, seek those who have fallen away, stand at the crossroads and welcome the outcast.[15]

---

13 *Redemptoris Missio*, 3.
14 St John Paul II, Message to World Mission Day, 20 October 1991.
15 *Evangelii Gaudium*, 24.

The evangelising initiative is Christ's. But Christ now acts in and through us. We are encouraged to "boldly take the initiative" as we go out in the Lord's name to make disciples. We have to share with others, in the words of the Second Vatican Council, "reasons for living and for hope".[16] The human heart longs to know these reasons.

St John Paul II reminds us that:

> The effectiveness of the Church's organizations, movements, parishes and apostolic works must be measured in the light of this missionary imperative.[17]

All the organisations in your parish should have as their ultimate aim the spreading of the Gospel. That is how the community becomes as merciful as our heavenly Father.

Embracing our true identity

Jesus said: "One does not live by bread alone, but by every word that comes from the mouth of God" (Matthew 4:4). When we live by God's word spoken to us about ourselves, we begin to see ourselves as God sees us. Pope Francis recalls a forgotten dimension to our Christian identity: all of us are missionary disciples of Jesus Christ. As we embrace our true identity as missionary disciples we begin to see ourselves as God sees us and we begin to take new hope for the future of the Church of Christ. The future does not simply depend on having more priests, religious sisters, and brothers, but on encouraging each baptised member of the Church to assume their true identity as missionary disciples. All of us together, lay faithful, priests and religious are Christ's missionary disciples in the twenty-first century.

Sometimes it is easier to see ourselves through the eyes of our critics and live by their words than it is to see ourselves as God sees us and live by his word. What life-giving words does God speak to us about

---

16 Second Vatican Council, *Gaudium et Spes* (Pastoral Constitution on the Church in the Modern World), 31.
17 *Redemptoris Missio*, 49.

ourselves? We don't have to guess because throughout the Bible God tells us. Let us consider just a few of those amazing words in which God reveals to us who we truly are and how God sees us.

Image and likeness of God

The very first thing God tells us about ourselves is that we are made in God's "image" and "likeness" (Genesis 1:26). There is nothing in the whole world more like God than us. We are off to a great start in life. But we must let this word sink into the depths of our being and live by it daily. As members of the Church we rejoice in believing God's revelation that we are made in God's image and likeness. But we also believe the same wonderful truth about every human being. The people you meet, work with, or who live in your neighbourhood are the image and likeness of God. It takes a spiritual effort to maintain this vision of ourselves and others and sometimes we may forget about it altogether. But, if we are not motivated by this revelation that we are made in God's image, we will never embrace our true identity as missionary disciples.

Fallen and redeemed

We believe, too, that our first parents disobeyed God. They sinned. This is a deep mystery. They were exiled from the Garden of Eden. But God didn't leave them without hope. He promised them a Saviour. We believe that the Lord Jesus Christ is the fulfilment of that promise. Our faith is our personal relationship with Jesus Christ. We believe that he is with us always and that he gives new meaning to our lives. As Pope Benedict XVI said:

> Being Christian is not the result of an ethical choice or a lofty idea, but the encounter with an event, a person, which gives life a new horizon and a decisive direction.[18]

This encounter is very personal and intimate. We cultivate it as the most precious friendship in our lives. And we take every opportunity

---

18   Pope Benedict XVI, *Deus Caritas Est* ("God is Love"), 1.

to help others to have the same experience of salvation. As Pope Francis says:

> If we have received the love which restores meaning to our lives, how can we fail to share that love with others?[19]

Our society has, as we know, almost demanded, as a spurious mark of courtesy and respect, the total privatisation of religion. You can talk about everything else, even your most intimate experiences, but don't talk about God or Christ or faith! We have to expose this spurious attitude to life.

Precious in God's sight

Despite their sinfulness and their infidelity to his covenant, the Father never changed his mind about the people he had chosen as his own in the Old Testament. He never loved them less because of their unfaithfulness. He sent them prophets to assure them of his unfailing love. The Lord said to them, "I have loved you with an everlasting love; therefore I have continued my faithfulness to you" (Jeremiah 31:3). And he assured them that they were precious in his sight:

> Do not fear, for I have redeemed you; I have called you by your name, you are mine... Because you are precious in my sight, and honoured, and I love you... Do not fear, for I am with you.
>
> Isaiah 43:1. 4. 5

God assures us too with those same words. No matter what our situation, no matter how often we fail to live in faithfulness to God's new covenant with his people, we are confident that we are precious in God's sight. As Pope Francis often says, "God never ever tires of forgiving us... we get tired of asking for forgiveness".[20] Even in our weakest and most sinful moments we can draw close to God, who loves to forgive and renew us in great mercy and love. Because we are sons and daughters of God we can always come into this loving presence.

---

19 *Evangelii Gaudium*, 8.
20 Pope Francis, Angelus, 17 March 2013.

Little less than a god and crowned with glory and splendour

In the beautiful psalm God assures us that we are "little less than a god", that we are "crowned... with glory and splendour" (Psalm 8:5). These are spiritual gifts. We don't see them in ourselves but God sees them in us because God has placed them there. We, in our turn, must train ourselves to see these gifts in others. There is nobody born into this world that God does not bless with gifts. The Second Vatican Council gives us the reason for God's loving regard for every human being. It teaches; "By his incarnation, he, the Son of God, has in a certain way united himself with each individual".[21] Just as Christ, the good Samaritan, never passes by but always reaches out to help those who are suffering and wounded, so we, when we are faithful to our true identity, will always be on the side of those who are lonely, lost, wounded and rejected.

Reborn of water and the Holy Spirit

Jesus outlined his purpose in coming into the world when he said, "I came that they may have life, and have it abundantly" (John 10:10). He said that to receive this new life each of us has to be reborn. Speaking to Nicodemus he said, "Very truly, I tell you, no one can enter the kingdom of God without being born of water and Spirit" (John 3:5). That rebirth happened for us when we were baptised. The literal meaning of word "baptism" is to plunge, to soak in water. We are plunged into the living water of the Holy Spirit in our baptism and are born again as sons and daughters of God, members of Christ. St Paul tells us that "if anyone is in Christ, there is a new creation: everything old has passed away; see, everything has become new! All this is from God" (2 Corinthians 5:17-18). Each day we should rejoice in gratitude for the gift of being God's new creation. Now we are in touch with our true identity. We know who we are and we are confident to share our true identity with others.

---

21   *Gaudium et Spes*, 22.

Temple of the Holy Spirit

Because of our rebirth through water and the Holy Spirit we have become shares in "the divine nature" (2 Peter 1:4), divinised, and in St Paul's words we have become the temple of the Holy Spirit. He says to us, "Do you not know that your body is a temple of the Holy Spirit within you, which you have from God, and that you are not your own?" (1 Corinthians 6:19). Jesus has sent the Holy Spirit into our hearts. We have been sanctified and purified by this infilling with the Holy Spirit. In our darkest moments we can cry out "come Holy Spirit" and the Spirit, who is the forgiveness of sins, will come to our assistance. When we are uncertain about our true identity as God's sons and daughters it is most important for us to invoke the Holy Spirit and gratefully remember that we have been reborn "of water and Spirit". We have no grounds for doubting our true identity.

God's work of art.

St Paul speaks the encouraging word of God to us today, saying, "For we are what he has made us, created in Christ Jesus for good works which God prepared to be our way of life" (Ephesians 2:10). God, the divine artist, didn't make a mistake when he created us. And, like any good artist, God takes pride in his work. Despite all our sinfulness and our failures God doesn't give up on us. He renews his great promise in our lives:

> I will sprinkle clean water upon you, and you shall be clean from all your uncleannesses, and from all your idols I will cleanse you. A new heart I will give you, and a new spirit I will put within you; and I will remove from your body the heart of stone and give you a heart of flesh. I will put my spirit within you.
>
> Ezekiel 36:25-27

Each new day we have the opportunity of living a new life in God's presence, living in the true knowledge of who we are as God's beloved children.

As we begin to see ourselves as God sees us we are filled with awe and amazement at our human dignity. St John Paul II identified the nature of this amazement when he said:

> In reality, the name for that deep amazement at man's worth and dignity is the Gospel, that is to say: the Good News. It is also called Christianity.[22]

Our Surname is God

When we say we are the daughters and sons of God we are identifying our deepest reality, our true identity. Pope Francis highlighted this well when he said, "To put it simply: we bear God's surname, our surname is God... Here lies the root of the vocation to holiness!"[23] Children normally receive their surname from their father. As you come into God's presence in your prayer time, you are acknowledging that God is your Father; you definitely bear his surname; God acknowledges you as a son or daughter and assures you that you have an absolute right to come into his presence. As we worship in this presence we can ask for all our needs. With the words of Jesus, "go... and make disciples", ringing in our ears, we ask the Father for the light and the grace, the wisdom and the enthusiasm that we need to fulfil our mission.

God's unconditional love for us

Because we are sinful, Christ not only revealed that God is our Father, he also revealed to us the qualities of our Father: all loving, all merciful, compassionate, forgiving, comforting, consoling, encouraging, and many other endearing features that are summed up in this beautiful description by St John: "God is love. God's love was revealed among us in this way: God sent his only Son into the world so that we might live through him" (1 John 4:8-9). When we say, "God is love" we are not saying that God loves us as our parents, or spouses or friends love us. We are saying that God is infinite love,

---

22   St John Paul II, *Redemptor Hominis* ("The Redeemer of Man"), 10.
23   Pope Francis, Angelus, 1 November 2015.

that God loves us unconditionally, and that there is nothing we can do that will ever force God to stop loving us. We experience human love, which is a beautiful and life-giving experience. We can say that human love gives us an inkling of what divine love is like. But divine love is really unimaginable. It can be compared to the love of parents for their children, of spouses for one another, of brothers and sisters, of friends and so on. But, in reality, the love that God has for us remains a mystery.

The mystery of God's infinite love for each human being ever born into this world is beyond our comprehension. Not everyone shares our Christian faith but we believe that God gives to each person ever born into this world the equal opportunity of receiving eternal life. As St Paul wrote, God "desires everyone to be saved and to come to the knowledge of the truth" (1 Timothy 2:4), and writing to the Romans, he said, "God shows no partiality" (Romans 2:11). Christians are not God's favourites. God has given us the light of faith and in that faith we believe that we are God's sons and daughters. That is why we come into God's presence, speak to God in prayer, ask for all that we need and pray for the whole human race. God loves equally those who do not yet believe in Christ and those who do accept Jesus as their Lord and Saviour. The Second Vatican Council taught this very consoling doctrine:

> Since Christ died for everyone, and since all are in fact called to one and the same destiny, which is divine, we must hold that the Holy Spirit offers to all the possibility of being made partners, in a way known to God, in the paschal mystery. Such is the nature and greatness of the mystery of humankind as enlightened for the faithful by the Christian revelation.[24]

God offers everyone the possibility of being saved but invites us who believe in him to be ambassadors of salvation. As St Paul said:

---

24 *Gaudium et Spes*, 22.

"God is making his appeal through us; we entreat you on behalf of Christ, be reconciled to God" (2 Corinthians 5:20).

Ambassadors of Christ

Our ambassadorial work as missionary disciples begins within our own hearts. God has revealed wonderful, life-changing truths to us about ourselves and we have to begin to live those truths in our daily lives. The way we live our lives in our homes, the way we relate to each person we meet or work with, the way we accept each person, making allowances for their shortcomings and even at times their negative attitudes or hostility, proclaim non-verbally that we are living a new life which people begin to recognise as the Christian life. This in itself creates the question that the ancient pagan Romans had: "See how these Christians love one another"; how can these people be happy, obliging, tolerant and non-judgemental? The work of evangelisation begins as the other person meets a loving, non-judgemental, joyful person, who is more interested in them as a person than in making a convert.

Revelation

The only reason we believe in God our Father is because Jesus came to reveal the Father to us. He says:

> All things have been handed over to me by my Father; and no one knows the Son except the Father, and no one knows the Father except the Son and anyone to whom the Son chooses to reveal him.
>
> Matthew 11:27

We believe in God our loving Father, not because we are more intelligent or better than those who don't, but for this sole reason: Jesus has given us that revelation in our hearts. We do not keep this revelation to ourselves. Jesus has given us the light of faith. That is the light that he asks us to let shine. It is in and through that light of faith that we find our way joyfully into the presence of God in prayer.

We want to communicate the joy of knowing that we are God's sons and daughters to everyone. In God's presence, then, we know who we are – we are the sons and daughters of God our Father who takes delight in us. Now we are ready to fulfil our role as ambassadors of salvation. As St Paul VI prayed in his great letter on evangelisation:

> May the world of our time, which is searching, sometimes with anguish, sometimes with hope, be enabled to receive the Good News not from evangelizers who are dejected, discouraged, impatient or anxious, but from ministers of the Gospel whose lives glow with fervor, who have first received the joy of Christ, and who are willing to risk their lives so that the kingdom may be proclaimed and the Church established in the midst of the world.[25]

---

25 *Evangelii Nuntiandi*, 80.

Personal spiritual exercise for internalising the message of this chapter

- Find a quiet place as free of interruptions and disruptions as possible: no TV or radio in the background, mobile phone on silent, etc. Sit in a comfortable chair, with your spine upright, your two feet firmly on the floor, your hands relaxed on your knees.

- Close your eyes. Begin to breathe deeply and rhythmically, inhaling deeply and slowly exhaling. Don't hold your breath.

- As you begin to feel stillness, Jesus Christ is with you as you cross the threshold into God's holy presence. Your brother Christ is now presenting you to God, his Father and yours.

- In God's presence, let go of all anxieties, worries and tensions. A traditional prayer may help: "Into your hands, O Lord, I commend my spirit."

- Now, in your stillness, allow one theme from the chapter to enter your mind: "I am made in the image and likeness of God," or, "my surname is God," or, "I am Christ's missionary disciple."

- Allow that one theme to fill your heart as you breathe in and out.

- Listen in your heart to God.

- After about ten minutes bring your thoughts back to where you are on your chair, in your room, and thank God for your time of silence in his holy presence.

- Now continue with your daily routine.

This technique for contemplation and deep relaxation may be familiar to you. It should leave you calmer and more aware of yourself as God's son or daughter and fill you with peace in body, mind and spirit. It is an excellent daily exercise for deepening your spirituality of proclaiming the Gospel.

— Chapter 2 —

The Church's deepest identity

The Catholic Church exists in every country in the world but she is not like an international, corporate organisation concerned just for her own members. Nor is the Church, as Pope Francis is fond of saying, a big NGO, a non-governmental organisation, helping people in need all over world – even though the Church provides more help through her members who teach, nurse the sick, feed the hungry, care for orphans and the elderly and work for human development on every level than all the NGOs put together. While providing all these services to humanity the Church never forgets that she exists to proclaim the salvation that Christ has gained for the whole world.

The mercy of Christ

The Second Vatican Council gave us this definition of the Church which is easy to remember: "The universal church is seen as 'a people made one by the unity of the Father, the Son and the Holy Spirit'".[26] This unity in Father, Son and Holy Spirit is the hallmark of the Church: we are God's people who have been redeemed by Jesus Christ; we share Christ's love with one another; we seek to make Christ known to others as we live and show forth that unity which we have with the Father, the Son and the Holy Spirit. Where the Church exists, Christ is present. Jesus made this great promise to his disciples as he sent them forth to the whole world to preach the gospel: "And remember, I am with you always, to the end of the age" (Matthew 28:20). This abiding presence of the redeeming Christ makes the Church "the sacrament of God's mercy" in the world today. In encountering the Church, the people of God, individuals and whole communities, should be encountering the mercy of God. As Pope Francis says:

---

26   Second Vatican Council, *Lumen Gentium* (Dogmatic Constitution on the Church), 4.

> Mercy is the very foundation of the Church's life. All of her pastoral activity should be caught up in the tenderness she makes present to believers; nothing in her preaching and in her witness to the world can be lacking in mercy. The Church's very credibility is seen in how she shows merciful and compassionate love. The Church "has an endless desire to show mercy". Perhaps we have long since forgotten how to show and live the way of mercy.[27]

Mercy should be the public face of the Church of Christ because he is the "face of the Father's mercy".[28] If people do not feel embraced by mercy as they approach the Church, they will never enter into communion with the Church. Our challenge is this: people meet the Church through her individual members in the parishes, in priest and people. As members of the Church, our witness to those who are seeking Christ and a deeper meaning in life should speak clearly about the mercy of God for each individual, no matter what their circumstances may be. We never sit in judgement nor indulge in condemnation, because we too remain sinners, always in need of God's mercy. The Church is often dismissed as living in the dark ages because of her strict code of morality and, at the same time, criticised by the very same voices for the extravagance of the mercy she shows to poor sinners who repent. Deep within our hearts we keep the words of Jesus to the scribes and Pharisees who were demanding that he would agree that a woman should be stoned for adultery: "Let anyone among you who is without sin be the first to throw a stone at her" (John 8:7). As the minister of God's mercy, the Church embraces with mercy each repentant sinner.

To be a Catholic

The statement "we are Catholics" can mean many different things. It can mean that we were baptised, educated in a Catholic school, brought up in a Catholic family, became a Catholic later on in life,

---

27 *Misericordiae Vultus*, 10.
28 *Misericordiae Vultus*, 1.

that we say our prayers and go to Mass every Sunday. Is that what it really means to be a Catholic? As we ponder this in our hearts we begin to hear the words of Jesus: "All authority in heaven and on earth has been given to me. Go therefore and make disciples of all nations" (Matthew 28:18-19). Making disciples is the mission statement of the Church. The Church exists to make disciples. Each diocese and each parish within the diocese has, on Christ's authority, the right and the duty to make disciples. We can't leave that to the priest or the deacon or the youth minister. It is to us that Christ says "proclaim the good news to the whole creation" (Mark 16:15). If our parish is not actively seeking to proclaim the good news of Christ to those outside its own members it will not pass the test set by St John Paul II:

> The effectiveness of the Church's organizations, movements, parishes and apostolic works must be measured in the light of this missionary imperative.[29]

Witness to Christ

It is through each one of us as individual members of the Church that people encounter the Church and experience the merciful welcome of Christ. We are witnesses to the love and mercy of Jesus Christ for each human being by the way we live and relate to them. Recalling the words of Pope Benedict XVI recounted in chapter 1:

> We become witnesses when, through our actions, words and way of being, Another makes himself present.[30]

Another becomes present! Christ becomes present to others as we seek to witness to him, not through eloquent words, but through the love that we have in our hearts for each person. We welcome all, both those who are seeking the truth and the meaning of their life and those who may be hostile to us. The bigger the sinner, the bigger the welcome! We are not a Church that condemns others; we are a

---

29 *Redemptoris Missio*, 49.
30 *Sacramentum Caritatis*, 85.

Church that encourages everyone, a Church that believes that the Father, who has been patient and forgiving in the way he deals with us, will be equally patient and forgiving with every single person, even with those who, at the present, may seem to be enemies of the Church. It is always worth reminding ourselves that there was a time when St Paul, who was known as Saul to the early Christians in Jerusalem, was the biggest enemy of the Church. Writing from his prison cell, towards the end of his life, to St Timothy, his disciple and helper, St Paul said:

> I was formerly a blasphemer, a persecutor, and a man of violence. But I received mercy because I had acted ignorantly in unbelief, and the grace of our Lord overflowed for me with the faith and love that are in Christ Jesus. The saying is sure and worthy of full acceptance, that Christ Jesus came into the world to save sinners – of whom I am the foremost. But for that very reason I received mercy, so that in me, as the foremost, Jesus Christ might display the utmost patience, making me an example to those who would come to believe in him for eternal life.
>
> 1 Timothy 1:13-16

Paul says that the mercy he received brought about that amazing spiritual transformation that changed him from being Saul, the persecutor of all Christians, to being St Paul, the apostle of the Gentiles. We learn from this that the Church's first witness in our world is to show love and mercy to all. If the Christian community can welcome into its midst the converted persecutor, Saul, and begin to revere him as the great St Paul, we despair of nobody's conversion. Everyone is welcome in the Church of Jesus Christ.

Love and mercy are not abstract terms but concrete virtues. We don't love humanity, nor have compassion for humanity. We love the individual person whom we encounter, the neighbour, and we have compassion for the individual suffering person whom we can help. The fact that I cannot help every suffering person at this moment is no justification for me not trying to help the person who turns to me for help. Each of us, by the way we live and respond to others, extends a welcome in the name of Jesus. No one is excluded because of their past. Once they open their hearts to Christ in the present, as Paul did, and seek the grace to put their trust in him in the future, they have been reconciled to God. The Church is not an elite club for sinless people. We will always remain a Church of sinners for sinners. Pope Francis profiles the type of Christians who are needed today:

> We need Christians who make God's mercy and tenderness for every creature visible to the men and women of our day. We all know that the crisis of modern man is not superficial but profound. That is why the New Evangelization, while it calls us to have the courage to swim against the tide and to be converted from idols to the true God, cannot but use a language of mercy which is expressed in gestures and attitudes even before words.[31]

If we are going to be merciful, just as our Father is merciful we cannot close our hearts to those in need. The mercy that we ourselves have received from God must be shared with those who need to receive our mercy. St John Paul II was very specific on this point:

> Jesus Christ taught that man not only receives and experiences the mercy of God, but that he is also called "to practice mercy" towards others: "Blessed are the merciful, for they shall obtain mercy." The Church sees in these words a call to action, and she tries to practice mercy.[32]

Reclaiming our true identity as a Church

When St Paul VI spoke about the identity of the Church he went beneath all the externals. He didn't dwell on all the good works

---

31   Address to Pontifical Council for Promoting the New Evangelization, 14 October 2013.
32   St John Paul II, *Dives in Misericordia* ("Rich in Mercy"), 14.

carried out by members of the Church all over the world: works that are called "the corporal works of mercy". He said:

> Evangelizing is in fact the grace and vocation proper to the Church, her deepest identity. She exists to evangelize, that is to say, in order to preach and teach, to be the channel of the gift of grace, to reconcile sinners with God, and to perpetuate Christ's sacrifice in the Mass, which is the memorial of His death and glorious resurrection.[33]

Highlighting evangelisation as the deepest identity of the Church, St Paul VI was preparing the Church to embark on the new evangelisation. Paul became pope on 21 June 1963, in the middle of the Second Vatican Council. He saw that the renewal of the Church – which was the aim and purpose of the Council – would be achieved only through fidelity to her deepest identity. The canonisation of Pope Paul VI should encourage us all to study again his great Apostolic Exhortation, published in 1975, ten years after the Second Vatican Council. This exhortation inspired the whole Church, beginning with St John Paul II, and inspiring Pope Benedict XVI and Pope Francis. Pastors of other Christian denominations found his exhortation very enlightening and helpful. Fr Gino Henriques, an Indian Redemptorist who has been engaged internationally in the ministry of evangelisation, shared this story with me. Around 1985 he was travelling on a plane from Korea to Singapore with three pastors of an evangelical church. They had been speaking at a conference in Korea on evangelisation. When they heard about his commitment to evangelisation they shared with him their presentation texts. To his delight all three quoted St Paul VI in their presentations. For them evangelisation was also the deepest identity of the Church. But for a number of years after the Second Vatican Council St Paul VI's great exhortation wasn't studied much by Catholics. St John Paul II's focus on the need for the new evangelisation

---

33   *Evangelii Nuntiandi*, 14.

in our time helped the Church to refocus on the major contribution that St Paul VI made. St Paul VI should be the patron saint of the new evangelisation.

Our missionary community

Our deepest identity as the Catholic Church is found not in beautiful churches and ceremonies but in the faith-filled act of sharing the good news of Jesus Christ with others. We don't wait for them to come to us. We go to them. We are sent by Christ with the mandate to bring the Gospel of salvation to others. We do this, not as isolated individuals, but as a community, as the assembly of God's people. If we are not evangelising as a Church we are not fulfilling the very purpose of our existence. It is worth repeating St John Paul II's words:

> No Christian community is faithful to its duty unless it is missionary: either it is a *missionary community* or it is not even a *Christian community*.[34]

I am sure you would agree that John Paul's words are very challenging. Are we a "missionary Church"? Is your parish a "missionary parish"? We have to seriously ask ourselves, as Catholic parish communities, how do we engage in the work of evangelising those who are not yet Christians and re-evangelising those who, although they have been baptised and confirmed, have ceased all practice of their faith?

A radical conversion in thinking

Each of us, in our own way, using the gifts that God has given us, can speak the word that will open the door to faith for the individual who is searching for God. Within your parish community today, as the Church keeps reminding us, there should be a growing consciousness of the urgent need to become involved, as a community, in the new evangelisation. Can your parish reassert its deepest identity as the

---

34   St John Paul II, Message to World Mission Day, 20 October 1991.

Catholic Church and become involved in the new evangelisation? St John Paul II says that we all have to undergo a radical conversion of thinking before we will commit ourselves to the new evangelisation. He wrote:

> A radical conversion in thinking is required in order to become missionary, and this holds true both for individuals and entire communities. The Lord is always calling us to come out of ourselves and to share with others the goods we possess, starting with the most precious gift of all – our faith.[35]

The Lord is certainly calling your parish to seek out new ways of sharing the good news of Jesus Christ with everyone in your neighbourhood. Maybe you could begin a conversation within your parish about how you could respond to the Lord's call? Test it out with a few parishioners who share your concerns about preaching the Gospel and reaching out to the lapsed and non-churched. The number doesn't have to be large because, as Jesus says to us, "Truly I tell you, if two of you agree on earth about anything you ask, it will be done for you by my Father in heaven. For where two or three are gathered in my name, I am there among them" (Matthew 18:19-20).

In Britain we have several thousand Catholic parishes. Each parish should have as its pastoral priority "the new evangelisation". We cannot be satisfied with the fact that our parish is merely "a good practising parish". If it is not evangelising, it is not yet fully converted. The parish has to seek out ways for its members to undergo this "radical conversion in thinking" that St John Paul II called for. One good way is the celebration of a "parish mission". This was the traditional means for parish conversion in the past thousand years. When I am preparing a parish for a week of parish mission I always emphasise that the purpose of the parish mission today is to enable the practising parish to become an evangelising

---

35 *Redemptoris Missio*, 49.

parish. At the end of the week's parish mission I have a gathering of parishioners on the Saturday morning to reflect on this question: *How is our parish evangelising the neighbourhood?* Normally there is a good turnout of men and women for this evaluation. They have very honest and frank discussions about what they need to do as a parish to reach out, not just to the lapsed in their midst, but also to non-believers. They fully accept what St John Paul II said to the Bishops of Oceania:

> All renewal in the Church must have mission as its goal if it is not to fall prey to a kind of ecclesial introversion.[36]

Becoming missionary is the way in which we can reveal the "Church's deepest identity". What would an evangelising parish look like?

Christ takes the initiative

We take our initiatives: we meet, discuss, decide and then we act. But all the time we believe that the evangelising initiative is Christ's. We listen again to the words of Pope Francis:

> An evangelizing community knows that the Lord has taken the initiative, he has loved us first (cf. 1 John 4:19), and therefore we can move forward, boldly take the initiative, go out to others, seek those who have fallen away, stand at the crossroads and welcome the outcast.[37]

It is Christ who commissions the Church to go and preach the Gospel. That is our great commission. But Christ now depends on us because it is through us that he continues to act in the world. Well-known words often attributed to St Teresa of Avila, though they are not found in her writings, express this extraordinary dependence of Christ on us in this way:

---

36 St John Paul II, *Ecclesia in Oceania* ("The Church in Oceania"), 19.

37 *Evangelii Gaudium*, 24.

Christ has no body now but yours. No hands, no feet on earth but yours. Yours are the eyes through which he looks with compassion on the world. Yours are the feet with which he walks to do good. Yours are the hands through which he blesses all the world. Yours are the hands, yours are the feet, yours are the eyes, you are his body. Christ has no body now on earth but yours.

St Paul would be happy with those words. He emphasises in all his letters this wonderful mystery that we are the Body of Christ in this world. He wrote: "Now you are the body of Christ and individually members of it" (1 Corinthians 12:27). That is why we are encouraged to "boldly take the initiative" as we go out in the Lord's name to make disciples. The important thing is that the parish is taking the initiative and not leaving the whole work of evangelisation to others. As the deepest identity of the universal Church is evangelisation, so too, the deepest identity of the local church, your parish, is evangelisation.

Reasons for living and for hope

The Second Vatican Council began on the 11 October 1962. Five days later, the 16 October, the Cuban missile crisis began. For eight days the world held its breath and feared some kind of nuclear catastrophe as the tension mounted between the two great nuclear powers, the USA and the Soviet Union, but by God's grace, wisdom prevailed and a political solution was found. This crisis was a learning experience for the bishops as they began their work of the Council. In the great document *Gaudium et Spes*, promulgated by the Council on 7 December 1965, we get a hint that they had that major crisis in mind when they said:

> One is right in thinking that the future of humanity rests with people who are capable of providing the generations to come with reasons for living and for hope.[38]

---

38 *Gaudium et Spes*, 31.

People today are searching for meaning in their lives. They need hope as they look to the future. The scourge of what is called relativism has robbed them of the hope of ever finding the truth. Truth, they are told, is relative. What is true for one person is not necessarily true for another person. They are told that there is no such thing as the truth. We are living in what is often called "the post-truth age". But Jesus says to us, "I am the way, and the truth, and the life. No one comes to the Father except through me" (John 14:6). What better reason for living and hoping can we give to people than to assure them that they have a loving Father in heaven, who listens to their cries for help, who is aware of all their struggles, and who loves them with such unimaginable love that he sent Jesus Christ to save them? All they have to do to find the truth they are yearning for is to open their hearts and invite Jesus Christ who is the Truth, to enter their lives. And we can assure them that if they ask for this gift of faith they will not be disappointed.

New outreach movements in the Church don't normally begin with big numbers. A small group, open to the Spirit, persevering in prayer, is all that is needed for God to begin a new missionary movement in the Church. In the next chapter you will read about Mothers Prayer Movement which began with two grandmothers meeting to pray for their grandchildren and has now spread to over a hundred countries.

Making disciples

Discipleship is a way of life, lived in the full awareness and acceptance of Jesus Christ as our Lord and Saviour, and in the joyful acceptance of his invitation to live a life of love and to be merciful just as his heavenly Father is merciful. Fr James Mallon writes:

> To be a disciple is to be a learner. To be a disciple of Jesus Christ is to be engaged in a lifelong process of learning from and about Jesus the master, Jesus the teacher. The English term "disciple" comes from the Latin *discipulus,* and provides the connotation that the learning process is

not haphazard, but intentional and disciplined. To become a disciple is to commit to such a process of growth.[39]

The disciple has met his master. The Christian disciple has a personal relationship with the Lord Jesus Christ. He doesn't just know about Christ, he knows Christ in his heart. As disciples we never stop learning. It is Jesus himself who asks us as his disciples to learn from him: "Learn from me; for I am gentle and humble in heart" (Matthew 11:29). That is the first lesson the disciple has to learn, namely, to be gentle and humble with everyone, and especially with those who may seem to have lost their way in life. Those who cannot be gentle and humble in heart as they approach others are not yet ready to be evangelists. They need to come to Jesus in prayer and ask him to teach them how to be gentle as he is gentle. He will not fail them. They will acquire the virtue in abundance.

Good news

We have good news – great news – for people today but we have to share it with gentleness and humility. We do not have the answers to everything but we can tell others the truth about how God sees and loves them, a truth that will lift them out of depression, fear and self-rejection and transform their lives. But first we must embrace this truth ourselves. That is why in the last chapter we explored our true identity, reminding ourselves that "our surname is God". We have to hold on to this conviction in our hearts. It is the antidote to the poison of the false humility that says I should not speak about God to anyone because I am unworthy and I have to struggle every day trying to live the Gospel. But we believe that Christ takes away our sins and that "the Spirit helps us in our weakness" (Romans 8:26), and so we have the confidence to speak about Jesus Christ to others. When we humbly turn to Christ and ask his help, it is he himself who is speaking through us. St John Eudes, one of the great missionary disciples of Christ expressed this well:

---

39   Fr James Mallon, *Divine Renovation: bringing your parish from maintenance to mission* (New London, CT: Twenty-Third Publications, 2014), 20.

> Remember that our Lord Jesus Christ is your true head and that you are his members. He is to you as the head is to the members of the body; all that is his is yours. His spirit, his heart, his body, his soul, all his faculties, all are to be used by you as if they were your own, so that serving him you may praise him, love him, glorify him. For your part, you are to him as a member to the head, and he earnestly desires to use all your faculties as if they were his own for the service and glorification of his Father.[40]

People are turning to all kinds of "remedies" for their weaknesses such as drugs and alcohol, to internet pornography, to anything that promises them escape from their inner desolation. The parish community, the Body of Christ in the local area, knows that Christ is the answer; it cannot remain silent. The devil will try to silence Christ's missionary disciples by insinuating that they are ill prepared, not yet ready and that they should leave evangelisation to those who are better prepared. We resist this temptation by prayerfully reminding ourselves that we belong to Jesus Christ who dwells in our hearts; he is our head and we are the members of his body; when we speak in his name we surrender our voice to him so that he can speak God's word to others through us. Each of us has to share with others the grace of salvation that we have received from Christ. As evangelising is the deepest identity of the Church so it is our own deepest identity as missionary disciples. Christ has entrusted to us the good news of God's great love and mercy for each person and no one should be deprived of this great liberating truth.

The commitment of the laity

This is a time of great hope in the Church. St John Paul II took great heart from the growing number of the laity who are committed to the work of evangelisation. He wrote:

---

40 The Divine Office: Office of Readings for the feast of St John Eudes, 19 August.

> The commitment of the laity to the work of evangelization is changing ecclesial life, while particular churches are more willing to meet with the members of other Christian churches and other religions, and to enter into dialogue and cooperation with them. Above all there is a new awareness that *missionary activity is a matter for all Christians*, for all dioceses and parishes, Church institutions and associations.[41]

That phrase "changing ecclesial life" means changing the way we begin to think about what it means to be Church. The awareness that *"missionary activity is a matter for all Christians"* has introduced a major change in the way we look at what it means to be a missionary Church. As we saw in the last chapter, religious orders and congregations of men and women devoted their apostolic zeal to the missions while the lay faithful supported them in every way they could. Evangelisation was not really the direct responsibility of the laity. Now St John Paul II can boast about "the commitment of the laity to the work of evangelization" changing the life of the Church. Lay organisations in the Church were mainly devoted to the corporal and spiritual works of mercy though some, like the Legion of Mary, were directly involved in evangelisation.

The witness of lay organisations in the Church

Throughout the ages, and especially in our own times, many Christian men and women have faithfully devoted their energies, their wealth, their time and their talents to engaging in works of mercy all over the world. St Mother Teresa became, in our own day, the iconic figure of these works of mercy. Many of our parishes have St Vincent de Paul Societies. We see their members after Mass, outside churches all over the country, with their collection boxes. The pound coins or the fifty-pence pieces that the Mass-goers put in those boxes feed a multitude of hungry people. It is so beautiful to see parents give

---

41 *Redemptoris Missio*, 2.

their children coins for the collection box. This is a true formation for the children in the works of mercy. Dr Michael Thio, President of the International Confederation of the Society of St Vincent de Paul, speaking about the Society's work at the Vatican in February 2013 gave the following report:

> Since our humble beginnings 180 years ago we are today present in 148 countries, with 780,000 members spread over 70,000 conferences, 1.3 million volunteers and serving over 30 million poor. The Society is involved in a wide range and variety of tasks and activities from the provision of food, clothing and necessities to the needy, homes for the poor and homeless, response to natural disasters in emergency reliefs and rehabilitation projects, assistance to refugees that emerged from political conflicts, engaged in systemic change programs in education, self-help projects, micro-financing, counselling and many others. Among many other assistance and projects for last year, special mention is made to emergency reliefs provided to over 20 countries affected by natural disasters along with rehabilitation projects, assistance in the Famine in the Horn of Africa, food and crops programs, provision for rebuilding, renovation and construction of houses and notably support for a project in the construction of an indoor playground of a kindergarten due to the Tsunami tragedy in Fukushima, Japan, that is subjected to nuclear radiation.[42]

Those 780,000 faithful missionary disciples give a glowing witness to Christ all over the world.

Another manifestation of the devotedness of the faithful to witnessing to Christ through generosity is Mary's Meals. A young Scottish layman, Magnus MacFarlane-Barrow, from his home in

---

42 Zenit.org, 1 February 2013.

the Scottish Highlands in 2002 began a charitable project which he called Mary's Meals. The purpose of this charity was to provide two hundred hungry children in Malawi with one cooked meal a day at school. He began his work in faith. Today, fifteen years later, Mary's Meals now feeds well over a million school children in a number of the poorest countries in the world. This has become possible through the generosity of thousands of men and women who give a few pounds to support this wonderful charity. Again, we see in Mary's Meals how missionary disciples of Christ find new ways of reaching out to the poor. To each of them Jesus says, "I was hungry and you gave me food" (Matthew 25:35).

Spiritual and intellectual formation of our lay evangelists

We witness the evangelising zeal of the laity in the many new apostolic and spiritual movements that have enriched the Church. As Bishop Barron writes:

> The "new movements" arose in the twentieth century primarily as a way to form and mobilize laity, so that they would see themselves as front-line carriers of the Church's mission. To date, the Vatican has granted canonical status to more than 120 of these movements, virtually all of them founded within the last hundred years.[43]

The Catholic Charismatic Renewal, Marriage Encounter, the Cursillo Movement, Teams of Our Lady, Couples for Christ, and the Mothers Prayer Movement are just a few of these new movements. St John Paul II was a great champion of all these new religious movements. Bishop Barron writes:

> He saw them as an eruption of the Holy Spirit in our time, and as a way of reviving the charismatic dimension of the Church alongside its institutional and bureaucratic

---

43 Robert Barron with John L. Allen, *To Light a Fire on the Earth: proclaiming the Gospel in a secular age* (New York: Image, 2017), 235.

structures. As an expression of that point John Paul adopted the custom of holding a major gathering of the movements in St Peter's Square in Rome on Pentecost Sunday.[44]

These groups, inspired by the Holy Spirit, form mature faith in their members. As St John Paul II said:

> The Evangelising activity of the Christian community, first in its own locality, and then elsewhere as part of the Church's universal mission, is the clearest sign of mature faith.[45]

The parish community can best respond to the call for a new evangelisation by providing for its members the opportunity of joining apostolic groups and organisations within the parish, the deanery or the diocese, that meet together on a regular basis, pray together, hear the word of God together, and learn together how best to bring the Gospel of Christ to others. This kind of spiritual formation cannot be provided by the Sunday Mass alone. While the homily during Mass is essential for ongoing spiritual formation, new initiatives are needed to help the good practising parish to become an evangelising parish. Without serious spiritual and intellectual formation in the parish, the parishioners will never have the confidence and the motivation to assume their true role as missionary disciples of Christ. Des Robertson in his excellent book expresses this well:

> While the Catholic Church has probably educated more people in its schools and universities than any other body on this planet to date, faith and ministry formation for anyone other than the clergy and religious effectively ends after Confirmation (if not after First Communion), and becomes limited to the Sunday homily. This is not

44 Barron, *To Light a Fire on the Earth*, 236.
45 *Redemptoris Missio*, 49.

enough for Catholics to proclaim the gospel in a free, well-educated, questioning society.[46]

Catholic schools make a great contribution to the education of Catholic children. The diocese and the parish must now urgently take responsibility for the ongoing formation of their parents and their grandparents in the faith and prepare them live the Church's deepest identity.

---

46 Des Robertson, *A Community of Disciples: making your parish all it can be* (New London, CT: Twenty-Third Publications, 2012), 3.

Personal spiritual exercise for internalising the message of this chapter

- Find a quiet place as free of interruptions and disruptions as possible. Centre yourself; sitting upright; breathing rhythmically; clearing your mind of all preoccupations.

- As you cross the threshold of stillness, you have come into God's presence.

- Let your heart be full of gratitude to God that you are a member of the Church, the Body of Christ in this world.

- In your heart entrust yourself, with all your joys and troubles, with all your good works and sinful weaknesses, to Christ our Saviour.

- Thank God the Father for sending us Christ his Son to redeem us.

- Now be still in the presence of the God of mercy and listen to Jesus your brother as he speaks in your heart and invites you to make him known to others.

- Allow *"Evangelisation is the deepest identity of the Church"* to sink deeply into your heart.

- Quietly say in your heart: "Lord, I accept your commission, but I need your Spirit."

- Focus again on your breathing as you relax in God's presence.

- Now bring yourself gently back to continue your daily routine.

This spiritual exercise will help you to personalise your understanding of evangelisation as the deepest identity of the Church.

— Chapter 3 —

Where does the motivation come from?

Have you ever noticed how people who have just experienced something wonderful, like the birth of their first child or the recovery from a serious illness, just have to talk about it? They have to tell their good news to their friends and share their joy with them. This very sharing of their joy not only increases their own joy but also fills their friends with joy.

Their experience of the new birth or the recovery is the motivation that impels them to share their good news. That impulse to share good news explains why missionary disciples, often in a very quiet and gentle way, feel impelled to share the Good News of the Gospel with others. St John Paul II said:

> The burning desire to invite others to encounter the One whom we have encountered is the start of the evangelising mission to which the whole Church is called.[47]

Those who have never experienced a personal relationship with Jesus Christ will find it difficult to tell others about what the Lord has done for them. Yet that is what Jesus asked the man he had set free from evils spirits to do. Let us read St Mark's unique account of this great exorcism by Jesus.

> They came to the other side of the lake, to the country of the Gerasenes. And when he had stepped out of the boat, immediately a man out of the tombs with an unclean spirit met him. He lived among the tombs; and no one could restrain him any more, even with a chain; for he had often been restrained with shackles and chains, but the chains he wrenched apart, and the shackles he broke in pieces;

---

47 *Ecclesia in America*, 68.

and no one had the strength to subdue him. Night and day among the tombs and on the mountains he was always howling and bruising himself with stones. When he saw Jesus from a distance, he ran and bowed down before him; and he shouted at the top of his voice, "What have you to do with me, Jesus, Son of the Most High God? I adjure you by God, do not torment me." For he had said to him, "Come out of the man, you unclean spirit!" Then Jesus asked him, "What is your name?" He replied, "My name is Legion; for we are many." He begged him earnestly not to send them out of the country. Now there on the hillside a great herd of swine was feeding; and the unclean spirits begged him, "Send us into the swine; let us enter them." So he gave them permission. And the unclean spirits came out and entered the swine; and the herd, numbering about two thousand, rushed down the steep bank into the lake, and were drowned in the lake. The swineherds ran off and told it in the city and in the country. Then people came to see what it was that had happened. They came to Jesus and saw the demoniac sitting there, clothed and in his right mind, the very man who had had the legion; and they were afraid. Those who had seen what had happened to the demoniac and to the swine reported it. Then they began to beg Jesus to leave their neighbourhood. As he was getting into the boat, the man who had been possessed by demons begged him that he might be with him. But Jesus refused, and said to him, "Go home to your friends, and tell them how much the Lord has done for you, and what mercy he has shown you." And he went away and began to proclaim in the Decapolis how much Jesus had done for him; and everyone was amazed.

Mark 5:1-20

Tell them all that the Lord in his mercy has done for you

That ex-demoniac became a great evangelist in his own countryside and city, telling everyone what Jesus had done for him. He simply told his neighbours and friends how Jesus delivered him from the evil spirits and restored him to full health in body, mind and spirit. His motivation to share with his friends flowed from his experience of what Christ had done for him. Speaking from one's own experience of what Jesus has done for oneself is always the most effective way of evangelising. It is called *witnessing*. St Paul VI emphasised the power of witnessing when he wrote:

> Modern man listens more willingly to witnesses than he does to teachers, and if he does listen to teachers, it is because they are first witnesses.[48]

When we speak about the Good News of Christ, about what God has done for us in Christ, we are not talking about ideas or abstract notions. We are speaking from our own experience of God's love and mercy, forgiveness and help. If we are not speaking from our own experience or willing to share our experience of God, we will find it hard to respond to a person who has every right to say to us, "If this God is so wonderful, tell us what he has done for you."

Alcoholics Anonymous groups

One of the most powerful and successful spiritual movements in the world is the Alcoholics Anonymous fellowship, known as AA groups. Thousands of men and women begin to regain their freedom from their alcoholic addictions by becoming members of this fellowship. On their website, Alcoholics Anonymous Great Britain introduces their approach to the addiction of alcohol in this way:

---

48 *Evangelii Nuntiandi*, 41.

> Alcoholics Anonymous is a fellowship of men and women who share their experience, strength and hope with each other that they may solve their common problems and help others to recover from alcoholism.[49]

"Sharing their experience" – that is where the power of the AA approach resides. They have discovered the power of personal testimony. During their meetings, as a member shares how he or she became sober and retained that sobriety, others receive new hope for their own struggles. The question begins to resonate in their hearts: "If he or she can become free again from such a powerful addiction, why not me too?" They begin the liberating Twelve Step Programme on their journey to freedom.[50] That is the motivating power of witnessing. Since the AA movement began in 1935, tens of millions of men and women all over the world have regained sobriety and lived happy and fulfilled lives.

Not surprisingly many spiritual movements today have adapted aspects of the Twelve Step Programme, especially the importance given to personal testimony to what the Lord in his mercy has done for them.

Baptism in the Spirit

In the past fifty years, ever since the Second Vatican Council, millions of Catholic men and women have been experiencing a great release in their spirits through the ministry of their Christian brothers and sisters. In their prayer groups or in the privacy of their homes they ask to be prayed with for a fresh infilling with the Holy Spirit. And God, who is always faithful to his promise, fills their hearts with great grace and gifts of the Spirit. This experience is often called "baptism in the Spirit" or "release in the Spirit". Their spirits come alive in new ways; they receive a new sense of God as their loving Father: they experience a more personal relationship with Jesus as their Lord and Saviour; they develop a deeper and more

---

49 www.alcoholics-anonymous.org.uk
50 For detailed information of this programme, Google "The Twelve Steps of Alcoholics Anonymous"

joyful awareness that they are the temple of the Holy Spirit who lives and works in them; they become hungry for the word of God and begin to read the scriptures with new eyes; prayer, especially the great prayer of the Mass, ceases to be just a duty and becomes the source of great joy and peace; they joyfully bring all their sins, failures, hurts and inner wounds to the Lord in the sacrament of reconciliation and experience deep healing as well as forgiveness; they become witnesses to Christ present in their family, in their parish and in the world. This experience of the Holy Spirit at work in their hearts gives them a new motivation to preach the Gospel. This is a powerful and often life-changing grace, one which each of us should humbly seek from the Lord each day. We can pray for this grace in our own words, asking Christ to fill us with his Holy Spirit and give us all the gifts of the Spirit that we need. Or you might find this prayer helpful because each part focuses on some special gift that we are asking from our Lord:

> Lord Jesus Christ, I accept you as my Lord, my Saviour and my King. I invite you to come afresh into my heart; forgive me all my sins; heal every wound of sin in my heart. Baptise me in your Holy Spirit; release within me all the gifts of the Spirit that I received in my baptism; fill me with your love and your peace because I want to be your faithful missionary disciple and witness to your gift of salvation for all.

I still remember with gratitude to God how on 24 September 1975, the feast of Our Lady of Mercy, I was prayed with by a priest I had never known, and received great blessings. At the time I was the director of our Centre of Renewal, Hawkstone Hall, in England. We had just organised our first three-month sabbatical renewal programme for priests and religious men and women. As the aim of the sabbatical was personal and spiritual renewal I had assembled a group of very talented theologians, men and women, to direct each week of the twelve weeks. I had read writings by Fr Francis Sullivan SJ, who was Dean of the Gregorian University in Rome, about the new spiritual renewal called, "the Charismatic Renewal" and how it was having a transforming effect in the lives of many men and women in the USA. I was, of course familiar with the charisms of the Spirit and had often given talks on these gifts. But I had never encountered a charismatic movement. While engaging a number of theologians in Rome and explaining to them my vision for the sabbatical programme, several of them suggested that I should visit Fr Sullivan. He received me most graciously. When he heard that the purpose of this new sabbatical course would be spiritual and personal renewal, he said he would be willing to help in any way he could. I asked him to direct a week on the Holy Spirit and his gifts on our first course. Then the Holy Spirit took over. One of the leaders of the new movement of charismatic renewal in England, Bob Balkam, an American who worked for Redemptorist Publications, knew Fr Sullivan. He knew that Fr Sullivan had been asked by the Holy See to investigate the charismatic renewal movement that was spreading throughout the Catholic Church in the USA. He also knew that Fr Sullivan had written a very positive evaluation of the movement and that St Paul VI had accepted it. Indeed, speaking about this renewal in May 1975 St Paul VI said, "How then could this 'spiritual renewal' not be a 'chance' for the Church and the world?". Bob asked me if he could bring a group of the "charismatic leaders" in England to Fr Sullivan's week. I agreed, but asked that they arrive on the Sunday, as the course would begin on the Monday morning. That Sunday afternoon thirty men and women, all experienced in this new movement of the Spirit, arrived at Hawkstone Hall. After the evening meal they had a prayer meeting and invited the participants of the sabbatical course to attend. That was my first experience of a charismatic prayer meeting. I was fascinated by the ease and simplicity with which those men and women prayed spontaneously, often breaking into songs of praise, and reading wonderful words of encouragement from the scriptures.

We heard a very powerful testimony of how the Lord had spiritually transformed one person's life. I was impressed by my first experience of this kind of prayer group.

On the Monday morning Fr Sullivan began his course. His lectures were well presented and theologically very enlightening. But the real charismatic actions were happening outside the lecture room. People were being prayed over by our visitors. They were telling the other members on the sabbatical programme that they had received great blessings of inner healing, gifts of peace and prayer and the grace to let go of deep resentments and forgive. Some were receiving physical healings for conditions of pain after receiving the grace to forgive from the heart. Every afternoon the Blessed Sacrament was exposed in the church for two hours. The momentum of prayer was beginning to engulf the whole sabbatical course. I was, of course, delighted for them and praised God for the graces that they were receiving. But I was still on the outside of the whole experience.

On the third day, during the exposition of the Blessed Sacrament, I became convinced that I could not stay on the outside any longer. I decided that I would ask the first priest I met after the exposition to come to my office, hear my confession and pray with me. The first one I met was a Fr Wilfrid Brieven, a Belgian priest who was secretary to Cardinal Suenens. St Paul VI had given Cardinal Suenens a special mandate to oversee the development of the Catholic charismatic renewal worldwide. Suenens had sent Fr Brieven to our centre to share in the course given by Fr Sullivan. I knelt in my office to make my confession to him. As soon as I had finished he began to pray. He imposed his hands on my head and shoulders, invoked the Holy Spirit to come, absolved me from all my sins and then continued to pray "in tongues". As he prayed I had an extraordinary sense of the Spirit filling my whole being, infusing me with a new joy and enthusiasm and confirming in me the conviction that this experience, this baptism in the Spirit, was for my ministry to others. I needed to be freed from all kinds of inhibitions that made it difficult for me to be spontaneous in prayer and to reach out and lay hands on the sick and pray for their recovery. I had never prayed with anyone in confession in the way Fr Brieven prayed with me, and no priest had ever prayed with me in that way either. Since that day I have always prayed with people who celebrate the sacrament of confession with me and many of them tell me that they experienced great inner healing. As I look back at that providential moment in my office over forty years ago, I see in it the source of my motivation for preaching the Gospel. We have the Good News of Jesus Christ's death and resurrection for our salvation to bring to others. We need the power of the Holy Spirit to bring the peace, joy and healing of Christ to those to whom we are called to minister.

What difference does the Holy Spirit make in our lives?

It is very helpful and indeed very necessary for us as missionary disciples to reflect on and become aware of this invisible, abiding presence of the Holy Spirit at work in the Church, in the world and in our hearts. The Spirit is the active memory of the Church; the teacher of our faith; "By his transforming power, he makes the mystery of Christ present here and now."[51] The Spirit is in the good works, the witness of Christians all over the world, as they seek to live the life of Christ; when we pray, it is the Spirit who prays in our hearts. To answer that question, "What difference does the Holy Spirit make in our lives?" the Orthodox Patriarch, Ignatius of Latikia in Syria, gave this very clear explanation in his address to the World Council of Churches:

> Without the Holy Spirit: God is far away, Christ stays in the past, the Gospel is a dead letter, the Church simply an organisation, authority simply a matter of domination, mission a matter of propaganda, liturgy no more than an

---

51 *Catechism of the Catholic Church*, 1092.

evocation, Christian living a slave morality. But with the Holy Spirit: the cosmos is resurrected and groans with the birth-pangs of the Kingdom, the risen Christ is there, the Gospel is the power of life, the Church shows forth the life of the Trinity, authority is a liberating service, mission is Pentecost, the liturgy is both memorial and anticipation, human action is deified.[52]

With Bishop Ignatius' clear teaching on the difference that the Holy Spirit makes in our lives, we will begin to understand more clearly what Jesus meant when he said, "it is to your advantage that I go away, for if I do not go away, the Advocate will not come to you; but if I go, I will send him to you" (John 16:7). We can now understand how the Holy Spirit is invisibly at work in our families and in our hearts each time we turn to God in prayer. In fact, we can only turn to God in prayer because the Spirit is already in our hearts.

The answer to all the materialisms of our age

St John Paul II, in his first encyclical letter to the Church, called us all to reflect more deeply on the gift of the Holy Spirit which makes us one with Christ and alive in Christ. He wrote:

> The present-day Church seems to repeat with ever greater fervour and with holy insistence: "Come, Holy Spirit!" Come! Come!... This appeal to the Spirit, intended precisely to obtain the Spirit, is the answer to all the "materialisms" of our age.[53]

St John Paul II's teaching that the appeal to the Spirit "is the answer to all the 'materialisms' of our age" is surely a word of encouragement that we should listen to afresh each day. It is very easy to lapse into

---

52 Ignatius of Latakia, Third World Assembly of Churches, July 1968; published in The Uppsala Report (Geneva, 1969), 298; cit. in Rupert Shortt, *God is No Thing* (London: Hurst and Company 2016), 67.

53 *Redemptor Hominis*, 18.

discouragement in the Church and in our society. Many things have gone wrong in our Church: great scandals have disturbed and upset the faithful of all ages; vocations to the priesthood and religious life in Britain and Ireland have dramatically decreased; many of our young people do not join the parish community for Sunday Mass; family life is being challenged and undermined in many ways; and, with so much violence in our world today, our societies have become much less peaceful and safe. Fresh encouragement is needed to face all these challenges. We can find that encouragement in St John Paul II's words. We have the answer to hand. We can invoke the Holy Spirit each day to come afresh on the Church, on our families, on our society and on ourselves. The Holy Spirit, as we say in the Creed, is "the Lord, the giver of life". As we invoke the Spirit to come, new life and new hope is given to us and to the Church. St Paul prayed this prayer for hope through the Spirit in his letter to the Romans: "May the God of hope fill you with all joy and peace in believing, so that you may abound in hope by the power of the Holy Spirit" (Romans 15:13). To abound in hope is the gift of the Holy Spirit, a gift that we need every day.

Prayer

Every missionary disciple I speak to tells the story of how the Holy Spirit empowered them and motivated them for their work of evangelising. The Charismatic Renewal is just one of the many forms of missionary initiatives inspired by the Holy Spirit in the Church today. Prayer always opens the door through which we have to enter into God's presence in order to be filled afresh with the Holy Spirit and receive the gifts we need for preaching the Gospel. We all need the support of at least a few like-minded and Spirit-filled brothers and sisters to persevere in prayer and the work of evangelising. Few of us are called to be hermits. Jesus assures us that we will get the support if we ask the Father for it. If there is little motivation in your parish for evangelisation, and nobody taking the initiative, maybe you and one or two others might begin to meet in the Spirit, to pray together and ask the Father in Jesus' name to release within you and within the parish a spirit of evangelising. You yourself will receive a great infilling of the Holy Spirit as you pray for others. We have a good example of how God blesses this kind of prayer in the story of Veronica Williams.

The Mothers Prayer Movement

In recent years a new prayer movement has spread throughout the world. It is known as the Mothers Prayer Movement.[54] Mothers and grandmothers, very aware of the pressures and dangers to which their children and grandchildren are exposed, be it drugs, internet pornography or violence, meet together in one another's homes or in some quiet place, to pray for their children and grandchildren. This initiative was taken by Veronica Williams and her sister-in-law, both grandmothers, in 1995. In an interview with Zenit.org, a Catholic internet news agency, Veronica explained how and why she started this movement. She had been collaborating with a group of Christians in Kent who were preparing a report for Parliament on what was happening to young people in our society. The title of the report was "What on earth are we doing to our children?" It was, as she said, full of statistics about drug abuse and other abuses and dangers. But she was very disappointed with the response from Parliament. She said:

> At the time I had nine grandchildren. I was so shocked when I read the report and I thought, what kind of society are my grandchildren growing up in? I wanted to do something but I felt very small against such big problems. But I just had a wonderful experience that made me understand the power of prayer, and of surrendering everything to the Lord. I decided I would pray for children, and my sister-in-law who knew nothing about my decision to pray, told me that she was woken up during the night and felt a call

---

54 I tell this story of Mothers Prayer Movement in my book *The Fountain of Grace: celebrating 150 years of the Icon of Love* (Chawton: Redemptorist Publications, 2015).

to pray for her children. For one month we prayed and meditated on the third joyful mystery of the Rosary (the Nativity of the Child Jesus) to ask Him what He wanted us to do. And in November 1995 with three other mothers we started praying for our children.[55]

That faith initiative that Veronica and her small group of mothers took in 1995, in the front room of her home in Kent, has now become a worldwide prayer movement with mothers and grandmothers meeting to pray for their children and grandchildren in a hundred countries worldwide. As Veronica said:

> We now have groups all over the world, probably 85% are Catholic, but there are mothers from different denominations: Pentecostals, Baptists, Anglicans, and Orthodox... And also some from other religions – Muslims and Hindus, and even atheists who come and find God. God is breaking down barriers.[56]

She describes the spirituality of the groups in this way:

> Our particular spirituality is based on giving everything to Jesus: we don't give advice to solve problems. We say: "I can't do it, Lord, but you can". This is the way we surrender totally to the Lord.[57] I know He opens doors. Miracles do happen. Children are coming back to faith in God, getting married, coming off drugs; children that have been missing are coming back home. Mothers experience a deeper personal experience with Christ, and come deeper into their traditional faith. Some that have left the Church have come back again.

---

55 Veronica Williams, "The 'Mothers Prayers' All Over The World", Zenit [Catholic online news agency], (8 March 2012) https://zenit.org/articles/the-mothers-prayers-all-over-the-world/, accessed 9 May 2018.

56 Zenit.org, 8 March 2012.

57 For a very clear and inspiring vision of surrendering to the Lord see *The Joy of Surrender unto Him* by Veronica Williams (Kent: The Solace Community, 2004). This little book explains the spirituality of the Mothers Prayers movement.

Veronica's list of the graces of Mothers Prayers read like a list of graces that would have been read out at the Perpetual Novena services in parishes all over the world for the last ninety years. God answers prayer. But Veronica's experience shows us, just as the millions who flocked to the Perpetual Novena showed us, that we need support, the support of the small intimate group of friends, in the front room of one's home, or of the larger parish community, to persevere confidently in our prayer.

Would you be willing to take the initiative and invite a friend or two to join you in prayer, asking the Lord to show you how your parish could grow from being a practising parish into an evangelising parish? If God has chosen people like Veronica Williams to do a mighty work of evangelisation, starting just in her front room, maybe he has a similar plan for you and a few of your friends? As you gather in prayer, asking Jesus to pour out the Holy Spirit afresh on you and guide you and your parish in the ways of evangelisation, doors will open, people will respond and God will show you the way he wants you to take. But we have to always pray with great patience and even greater hope. St Paul writes: "Pray in the Spirit at all times in every prayer and supplication. To that end, keep alert and always persevere in supplication for all the saints" (Ephesians 6:18). When we begin praying about evangelisation we become aware of our own weakness. By ourselves we cannot make Christ known. That is why St Paul urges us to "pray in the Spirit". He spelt this out very clearly when he wrote:

> The Spirit helps us in our weakness; for we do not know how to pray as we ought, but that very Sprit intercedes with sighs too deep for words. And God, who searches the heart, knows what is the mind of the Spirit, because the Spirit intercedes for the saints according to the will of God.
>
> Romans 8:26-27

Because the Holy Spirit is praying in our hearts we never give up and we remain hopeful as we await God's answer to our prayers.

Our motivation comes from our faith

Our Christian "faith" is, in the first place, our encounter with Jesus Christ. It is not a system of good laws, or good liturgy, or good theology, but the grace of getting to know the person of Jesus Christ. We discover personally that, when we open our heart to Jesus our Saviour, he frees us from all our sins and heals all the wounds of sin in our lives. He fills us with the Holy Spirit who gives us great peace. This is the very personal grace which Jesus refers to when he said "this is eternal life, that they may know you, the only true God, and Jesus Christ whom you have sent" (John 17:3). It is not knowing *about* God or *about* Christ in the way we know about historical figures in the past – God and Jesus Christ are not in the past – we know God and we know Christ in the present. We acquire this personal knowledge, not through our own intelligence, but through an inner revelation from God. We can say that we believe in God the Father and that we accept Jesus Christ as our Lord and Saviour only because Jesus has revealed these life-transforming truths to us. We don't believe in God our Father because we are more intelligent than those who don't. Without the light of faith we would not believe. Our faith is our personal, loving relationship with Jesus and with God the Father, made possible by the Holy Spirit dwelling in our hearts.

Two meanings of faith

The word "faith" has two quite distinct meanings for us. We talk about *the faith that we believe* and we also talk ab*out the faith by which we believe. The faith that we believe* is the doctrine, the teachings of the Bible and of the Church. A person can spend a lifetime studying the faith that we believe – this is what we call the study of theology. It is an important study. We learn more about the content of our faith and come to a deeper understanding of it. But knowing a great deal about our faith does not mean that we know Jesus Christ. I preached parish missions for a number of years with an English Redemptorist confrere who was born in India before it got its independence. He attended the Christian Brothers' school.

He would always tell the congregation, during a mission service, that the teaching of the doctrines of the faith was excellent in that school, but the boy who always came top of the class, who knew the answer to every catechetical question, was not a Christian but a Hindu boy. He would then point out the great difference between knowing about the faith and knowing Jesus Christ. We get to know about the faith, about the teachings of the Bible and the Church, when we apply our minds to study. It is a work of human intelligence. We can only know Jesus Christ through the light of faith, *the faith by which we believe*, the gift of faith in our hearts. When Jesus asked his disciples, "But who do you say that I am?" Peter responded, "You are the Messiah, the Son of the living God". How did Peter know who Jesus was? Jesus made it very clear to him. He said, "Blessed are you, Simon, son of Jonah! For flesh and blood has not revealed this to you, but my Father in heaven" (Matthew 16:15-17). Jesus tells Peter and us that only God the Father can reveal who Jesus Christ truly is. We know he is the son of his mother Mary. We would not know that he is also the Son of God if God the Father hadn't revealed this wonderful truth to us through the gift of *the faith by which we believe*.

Every Sunday during Mass we stand as a community and profess our faith in Jesus Christ. We say together, "I believe in God the Father almighty, creator of heaven and earth; and in Jesus Christ his only Son, our Lord; who was conceived by the Holy Spirit and born of the Virgin Mary." If someone were to ask you after Mass how you know all this about Jesus Christ, you should respond by repeating what Jesus said to Peter. The very fact that we believe that Jesus Christ is the Son of God means that God the Father has given us this revelation in our hearts. That is the gift and the light of faith.

It is that gift that we share. It is that light of faith that Jesus asks us to let shine: "Let your light shine before others, so that they may see your good works and give glory to your Father in heaven" (Matthew 5:16). Notice that Jesus doesn't ask us to say anything. Living in the light of our faith, in the full awareness that we are daughters and sons of God, and doing the good works that faith inspires us to do, speaks much louder than thousands of words. Those good works are works of love, and because they are manifestations of love, they begin to speak to observers about the goodness of God who is love. They speak also about the goodness that resides in the depths of the human heart, in the depths of their own hearts, which is the capacity to love.

Love is a gift of the true self

The Second Vatican Council said in a very enlightening statement:

> If human beings are the only creatures on earth that God has wanted for their own sake, they can fully discover their true selves only in sincere self-giving.[58]

That short sentence is a good definition of what we mean by love. Love is always self-giving, never self-seeking. Love is a gift of self to the other person. Each of us has the capacity to make that gift. And when we make that gift we make a great discovery. In the words of St John Paul II:

> We have "*the power to express love: precisely that love in which the human person becomes a gift and* – through this gift – fulfils the very meaning of his or her being and existence".[59]

Jesus asks us to love one another, to love even our enemies. It is that love, made manifest in the way we relate to others, that manifests God. That was the puzzle that these early Roman pagans had to struggle with: "See how these Christians love one another." And notice what happens when we love in that way. We fulfil the very meaning of our being and existence. J. Brennan Mullaney, a leading Christian therapist writes:

---

58 *Gaudium et Spes*, 24.
59 St John Paul II, *Man and Woman He Created Them: a theology of the body* (Boston: Pauline Press, 2006), 15:1.

> Love is the most elemental human need, the raw force of the psychospiritual heart from which is derived all emotion, all thought, all volition and all behaviour.[60]

Mullaney, from his experience as a therapist and his vast knowledge of the many theories and methods of psychotherapy, agrees with this profound teaching of St John Paul II:

> Humans cannot live without love. They remain a being that is incomprehensible for themselves, their lives are senseless, if love is not revealed to them, if they do not encounter love, if they do not experience it and make it their own, if they do not participate in it.[61]

This is the love that Jesus speaks about when he says to us: "Just as I have loved you, you also should love one another. By this everyone will know that you are my disciples" (John 13:34-35). The light of Christ shines through our loving actions, our loving kindness in the way we relate to others, our genuine, non-judgemental acceptance of each person.

Our very first act of evangelising others and sharing our faith with them is living a life of love for everyone, thus manifesting, by the way we live, that we are disciples of Christ. Evangelising work that is not a manifestation of true love is doomed to failure. Our experience of the inner peace that Christ instils into our conscience gives us the motivation to share the Good News with others. Our motivation is our love for our neighbour. There is no medicine for the broken heart, nor is there any medicine for the guilty conscience. Only Christ can heal the broken heart and fill our conscience with inner peace and joy. When you meet someone, perhaps a dear friend, in some kind of inner darkness and pain, you can let the light of your faith shine and give them new hope. The experience of the peace with which Christ fills you impels you at times to share with others what the

---

60 J. Brennan Mullaney, *Authentic Love: theory and therapy* (New York: St Pauls, 2008), 3.
61 *Redemptor Hominis*, 10.

Lord has done for you. That is the source of your motivation. This is good evangelisation. Can you imagine what would happen if every practising Catholic in your parish shared their faith with friends in need? Your practising parish would become an evangelising parish and the fruits of the Spirit, especially the fruits of love, joy and peace, would be evident to everyone.

Personal spiritual exercise for internalising the message of this chapter

- Find a quiet place as free of interruptions and disruptions as possible. Centre yourself; sitting upright; breathing rhythmically; clearing your mind of all preoccupations.

- As you cross the threshold of stillness, you have come into God's presence.

- Let your heart be full of gratitude to God that you are a member of the Church, the body of Christ in this world.

- In your heart entrust yourself, with all your joys and troubles, with all your good works and sinful weaknesses to Christ our Saviour.

- Thank God the Father for sending us Christ his Son to redeem us.

- Invite the Holy Spirit to come into your heart.

- Now be still in the presence of the God of mercy and listen to Jesus your brother as he speaks in your heart and invites you to be make him known to others.

- Now focus again on your breathing as you relax in God's presence.

- Now bring yourself gently back to continue your daily routine.

This spiritual exercise of relaxing in God's presence will help you to personalise your understanding of evangelisation as the deepest identity of the Church.

— Chapter 4 —

Preparing our hearts and minds for the work of the new evangelisation

A journey of a thousand miles begins with the first step and with the right attitude. This is often the most difficult step to take. We experience this difficulty when thinking about evangelising: Where do I begin? When should I begin? What will I say? Am I qualified to say anything about my faith in Christ? As we contemplate taking the first step on the road of the new evangelisation we can be assailed by a thousand doubts. We have to make sure that we have the right attitudes, the attitudes of Christ. Jesus says to all his missionary disciples: "Learn from me, for I am gentle and humble in heart" (Matthew 11:29). That is why in the first two chapters we tried to get in touch with our true identity as sons and daughters of God and with the deepest identity of the Church which is, in the words of St Paul VI, evangelisation.

The Church exists to evangelise

The Church exists to evangelise. She fulfils her mission through us, both as individuals and as members of our parish community. Each of us has been filled with the Holy Spirit, blessed with gifts of the Spirit, the charisms, for living our Christian life and sharing our faith with others. Our Church is the dwelling place of the Holy Spirit who directs, empowers and guides her in every age. St Paul VI wrote:

> Techniques of evangelisation are good, but even the most advanced ones could not replace the gentle action of the Spirit. The most perfect preparation of the evangeliser has no effect without the Holy Spirit. Without the Holy Spirit the most convincing dialectic has no power over the heart of man. Without him the most highly developed schemas

on a sociological or psychological basis are quickly seen to be quite valueless.[62]

It is the Holy Spirit who will give you and your parish the confidence to become involved in the new evangelisation. Our confidence must always be in the Spirit and in the guiding of the Spirit and not in our own abilities. As St Paul VI reminded us, while techniques are good, the success of the work of evangelisation depends on the action of the Spirit in the hearts of people and not on the skills of those who are evangelising. This, of course, doesn't mean that evangelisers don't have to prepare themselves for the work. It means that they will always judge their ability in the light of the Spirit's presence in their hearts. And, because they believe the Spirit wants them to prepare themselves as well as they can, they will willingly and joyfully undertake the necessary preparation.

When we calmly look at ourselves and look at our Church that is guided by the Holy Spirit we have no grounds for fear. Yet, I recognise that the devil will always try to instil that fear, whispering that we are not good enough, not learned enough, not committed enough to be missionary disciples. We have to turn a deaf ear to those whispers and allow the Lord to do for us what he did for the prophet Isaiah:

> The Lord God has given me the tongue of a teacher, that I may know how to sustain the weary with a word. Morning by morning he wakens – wakens my ear to listen as those who are taught. The Lord God has opened my ear, and I was not rebellious, I did not turn backwards.
>
> Isaiah 50:4-5

Each of us can give that word of comfort to the weary we meet on our journey through the joys and sorrows of this world. The Lord gives each of his missionary disciples the words that he wants them

---

62 *Evangelii Nuntiandi*, 75.

to speak. Very often, those words are non-verbal, like a smile or a helping hand, or a gentle courtesy, like allowing someone to go before you in the supermarket or giving some change and a kind word to a homeless person. These are acts of courtesy and generosity but they are also non-verbal words of love and respect for another human being in whom you see the image of God. And, if you listen well you will hear Jesus saying "Truly I tell you, just as you did it to one of the least of these who are members of my family, you did it to me" (Matthew 25:40). Evangelisation doesn't begin with words but with acts of love, care and respect. In fact, if these qualities are absent the words are empty.

Use words if necessary

If you have the desire in your heart to share the Gospel of Jesus Christ with others you are probably doing that already, though, perhaps, not in a verbal way. The great St Francis of Assisi is supposed to have said to his friars "go and preach the Gospel and use words if necessary". Although there is no record of St Francis ever speaking those words, the legend has lived on. Words are needed to explain why, as disciples of Christ, we try to live a life of love and service. But it is the life of love and service that attracts others in the first place and not our words. Living the Gospel life, living in love and forgiveness, in peace and gentleness, is the first and the most effective step we take on the road of the new evangelisation. As St Paul VI said:

> For the Church, the first means of evangelisation is the witness of an authentically Christian life given over to God in a communion that nothing should destroy and at the same time given to one's neighbour with limitless zeal... Modern people listen more willingly to witnesses than to teachers, and if they listen at all to teachers, it is because they are first witnesses.[63]

---

63 *Evangelii Nuntiandi*, 41.

The attraction of love and unity

As we have seen already, Pope Francis likes to emphasise this truth: "It is not by proselytizing that the Church grows, but by attraction".[64] If nothing about a parish community attracts the outsider, he or she will not be knocking on the door! What attracts is the attitude we have for people, often people we have never met before and people we might find hard to like. Each of us can ask ourselves, "Am I a warm, welcoming person as I approach people or do I emit signals of suspicion?" Approaching people with the right attitude, in the right frame of mind, is absolutely vital because that first encounter, that meeting with another person should communicate non-verbally, through the body language, welcome, respect, acceptance and genuine love for and interest in this brother or sister. This encounter in itself is the beginning of evangelisation. The other person has met a loving, non-judgemental, joyful person who is more interested in him or her, as a person, than in making a convert. In your parish there may be many people who will never open their mouths to proclaim the Gospel but through their whole attitude towards others they are powerful witnesses to Christ. Others, however, will reap the rich harvest that they sow by their witness when they proclaim what Christ has done. St Paul VI said that silent witness always needs explanation:

> Even the finest witness will prove ineffective in the long run if it is not explained, justified – what Peter called always having "your answer ready for those who ask you the reason for the hope that you all have" (1 Peter 3:15) – and made explicit by a clear and unequivocal proclamation of the Lord Jesus. The Good News proclaimed by the witness of life sooner or later has to be proclaimed by the word of life. There is no true evangelization if the name, the teaching, the life, the promises, the Kingdom and the mystery of Jesus of Nazareth, the Son of God, are not proclaimed.[65]

---

64 *Evangelii Gaudium*, 14.
65 *Evangelii Nuntiandi*, 22.

Listening

Our primary attitude is one of listening. If the person wants to talk about his or her life we listen respectfully, accept the sincerity of their sharing, and, if and when they invite us to share something about our own life's journey, we do so gently and humbly, never conveying the false sense that we have all the answers to life's questions. The redemption that we know in our own lives doesn't make us immune to life's struggles and disappointments. But it does give us a new way of living with these challenges. We have the grace to gratefully accept ourselves with all our weaknesses and to put all our confidence in God's great love and mercy. The encounter with the brother or sister on the road of life provides them with what Pope Francis called "an oasis of mercy", which we discussed in chapter 1.

In this encounter they should have the sense of having reached a safe place in life's desert – a place where they are non-judgementally listened to and are refreshed through the love and respect which gives them the sense of being unconditionally accepted for who they are, and where they are in their life's journey. They may be feeling very bad about their own lives, living in self-rejection. Our acceptance of them just as they are, our focusing on what is good in their lives, communicates the truth to their spirits, just as St Paul – the greatest of the evangelists – freely admitted that he was the one most in need of salvation.

We walk patiently with those who may be showing an interest in finding a deeper meaning in life or the healing of some deep hurt, and we resist the temptation to hasten the process and get to the real "meat" of evangelisation. We have to convince ourselves that true evangelisation has already begun in our sincere acceptance and through the love and respect that we have for them. We are building trust without which no spiritual relationship will develop and no evangelisation will come to fruition. Through our love and acceptance we are witnessing to Christ. As Pope Benedict XVI said:

The first and fundamental mission that we receive from the sacred mysteries we celebrate is that of bearing witness by our lives. The wonder we experience at the gift God has made to us in Christ gives new impulse to our lives and commits us to becoming witnesses to his love. We become witnesses when, through our actions, words and way of being, Another makes himself present. Witness could be described as the means by which the truth of God's love comes to men and women in history, inviting them to accept freely this radical newness.[66]

Through our love, respect and acceptance of the person, Christ himself becomes present. We are never alone in the work of evangelisation. Because Christ is present, we listen to him in our hearts and allow him to direct our dialogue. We may observe too how Christ begins to help the person to relax; he casts out fear; he opens the heart that may have been closed for years; fills the person with new hope. We may have no answers for the specific problems the person has at the moment but our love itself is more effective and affirming than all the answers we could possibly give. It is this love which enables the person to welcome this new relationship and seek further opportunities to continue the conversation.

Affirming the other person

The sensitive missionary disciple knows how to affirm the goodness in the other person before he or she ever speaks about God. Interest in the person, expressed in empathetic listening and good conversation, will eventually lead to the question of identity, to how this person sees self, accepts self, and loves self. At this stage the word of encouragement often releases a person's cry for meaning in life. For instance, just the simple remark like "You're a good person and you have being doing your best" may quickly get the response "But I was very unkind to my dad and now that he is dead I feel

---

66 *Sacramentum Caritatis*, 85.

very guilty and nothing I do can get rid of it." Now we have the cue for talking about salvation: about God's forgiveness; the healing of inner wounds; about Christ who came specifically to take away all our sins and to heal every wound in our hearts.

Notice the progression here. We begin by "[sustaining] the weary with a word", as the prophet Isaiah said; we acknowledge the person's goodness; we assure him or her that they were trying to do their best. They accept most of that but begin to talk about times when they know they did wrong, violated sacred relationships, and are now feeling guilty and crying out for a saviour. They have moved from "I am alright the way I am" to "I need help right now because of the way I am." They acknowledge that they need a saviour who can heal their hearts and give a new meaning to their lives. They are now open to hear the Good News of Christ. Genuine interest in the person is the key that opens the door to their heart. Our first concern is to get to know the person and, if he or she so desires, to walk a part of life's journey together. We want to know what they believe about themselves, the kind of person they feel they are. We help them to explore their own goodness, pointing out that doing a bad thing doesn't make a person a bad person. It manifests a weakness and the Holy Spirit comes to help us in our weakness.

Developing good attitudes

Missionary disciples have to train themselves daily to listen attentively to those who may be showing some interest in faith or religion or in Jesus Christ. They have to show them love, respect, and unconditional acceptance, even if at first they may appear hostile. We seek to wholeheartedly follow Christ's great commandments to love our neighbour and, indeed, to love our enemies, in order to become missionary disciples with good news to share. We have to purge our minds and hearts of all negativity. As missionary disciples we never engage in negative gossip about any one or any group. Negativity in the heart about anyone, and especially about those who may not respond to all our efforts at evangelising, is a real poison in the spirit. It can, of course, be disappointing, maybe even frustrating, if you have worked hard trying to interest a group in the Lord and get no response. But that should never cause you to be negative or sarcastic about any person or group. Jesus himself had the experience of receiving no response from certain groups, especially in his home town of Nazareth. This is how St Mark described the Lord's experience when he tried to preach the Gospel in the synagogue in Nazareth:

> He left that place and came to his home town, and his disciples followed him. On the sabbath he began to teach in the synagogue, and many who heard him were astounded. They said, "Where did this man get all this? What is this wisdom that has been given to him? What deeds of power are being done by his hands! Is not this the carpenter, the son of Mary and brother of James and Joses and Judas and Simon, and are not his sisters here with us?" And they took offence at him. Then Jesus said to them, "Prophets are not without honour, except in their home town, and among their own kin, and in their own house." And he could do no deed of power there, except that he laid his hands on a few sick people and cured them. And he was amazed at their unbelief.
>
> Mark 6:1-6

We have the mind of Christ

Christ's missionary disciples will also frequently be amazed at the lack of faith that some people show. But they never indulge in criticism or condemnation. They cultivate Christ's own attitudes. St Paul can say, "We have the mind of Christ" (1 Corinthians 2:16). As we think with "the mind of Christ" we will not go astray. But we have to constantly keep learning from him as he invites us with these words: "Learn from me for I am gentle and humble in heart"

(Matthew 11:29). As we cultivate the gentleness and humbleness of Christ we will not feel obliged to win every argument or be praised for everything we try to do. We will not take offence when people reject our efforts at evangelising. Those who would take offence are not yet spiritually mature enough to engage in evangelising. St Paul encouraged the Philippians with these words: "Let the same mind be in you that was in Christ Jesus" (Philippians 2:5). Seeking to live with the mind of Christ, we will be ready to calmly and lovingly reach out to everyone.

Learning from Christ how to give time to prayer

We know that the attitudes we have to bring to our work as missionary disciples must be the same attitudes that Jesus had. We can only develop those attitudes by imitating Christ, and especially learning from him to give good time to prayer. This was the special request the disciples made to Jesus after they were with him for some time. They had been carefully observing his every move and listening intently to every word he spoke. They knew that he gave a lot of time to prayer. St Luke is the evangelist who dwells most on Jesus at prayer. He writes:

> He was praying in a certain place, and after he had finished, one of his disciples said to him, "Lord, teach us to pray, as John taught his disciples." He said to them, "When you pray, say: Father, hallowed by your name…"
>
> Luke 11:1-2

Jesus taught them on that occasion his prayer, the Lord's Prayer, the Our Father. The disciples were now getting their first glimpse into how Jesus was praying. He was in the presence of his Father and he was having a loving conversation with his Father. That is how Jesus wanted them to pray. That is how Jesus wants us to pray. We too, when we pray, are in the presence of our Father. Like Jesus, we too can be having a loving conversation with our God. Pope Benedict XVI commented:

> The fact that Luke places the Our Father in the context of Jesus' own praying is therefore significant. Jesus thereby involves us in his own prayer; he leads us into the interior dialogue of triune love; he draws our human hardships deep into God's heart.[67]

The Lord's Prayer is a formation of both mind and heart. It is the great prayer of the Christian people of all the different Christian denominations. It forms within our spirits and hearts the awareness of who we truly are as sons and daughters of our heavenly Father. We should also be aware that in calling God our Father we are also including all the tenderness of God as Mother. The Catechism makes this helpful comment:

> By calling God "Father", the language of faith indicates two things: that God is first origin of everything and transcendent authority; and that he is at the same time goodness and loving care for all his children. God's parental tenderness can also be expressed by the image of motherhood, which emphasises God's immanence, the intimacy between Creator and creature.[68]

If the image of father doesn't speak to someone about the goodness and love of God, the image of mother may do so. In the scriptures God compares himself to a mother in this way: "You shall nurse and be carried on her arm, and dandled on her knees. As a mother comforts her child, so I will comfort you" (Isaiah 66:12-13). And in the psalms we read: "Like a little child in its mother's arms, like a little child, so I keep myself" (Psalm 131:2). Jesus, in revealing God to us as our Father, calls us into an intimate, trusting, loving relationship with our heavenly Father. Sadly, as Pope Benedict XVI pointed out, the image of father is not always a comforting one:

---

67 Pope Benedict XVI, *Jesus of Nazareth: from the baptism in the Jordan to the transfiguration* (London: Bloomsbury, 2007), 311.
68 *Catechism of the Catholic Church*, 239.

It is true, of course, that contemporary men and women have difficulty in experiencing the great consolation of the word father immediately, since the experience of father is in many cases either completely absent or obscured by inadequate examples of fatherhood.[69]

There can be a wound in the heart, a "father wound", a space left empty because of the absence of one's father, or the absence of a father's love, encouragement and compassion. But that wound in the heart of God's son or daughter will be healed if they bring it into God's presence and say, "Father, gracious Father, loving Father" and allow the Father's love to embrace them. While our earthly fathers may not have been perfect, our heavenly Father is full of love, mercy and compassion for each of us. The Lord assures us that he has come "to bind up the broken-hearted" (Isaiah 61:1).

The effectiveness of prayer

Jesus took the opportunity of being asked to teach his disciples how to pray to evangelise them on the effectiveness of prayer. He says:

So I say to you, Ask, and it will be given to you; search, and you will find; knock, and the door will be opened for you. For everyone who asks receives, and everyone who searches finds, and for everyone who knocks, the door will be opened. Is there anyone among you who, if your child asks for a fish, will give a snake instead of a fish? Or if the child asks for an egg, will give a scorpion? If you then, who are evil, know how to give good gifts to your children, how much more will the heavenly Father give the Holy Spirit to those who ask him!

Luke 11:9-13

Jesus didn't send his disciples out empty-handed to make disciples. He shared with them his own secret, his relationship with God his

---

69 *Jesus of Nazareth*, 135.

Father, and with the Holy Spirit. Jesus guarantees us that when we ask the Father for the gift of the Holy Spirit we will receive that gift; the Holy Spirit will come afresh into our lives when we pray. Jesus knew that from his own experience. St Luke tells us what happened when Jesus was at prayer after his baptism in the Jordan River by John the Baptist:

> Now when all the people were baptised, and when Jesus also had been baptised and was praying, the heaven was opened, and the Holy Spirit descended upon him in bodily form like a dove. And a voice came from heaven, "You are my Son, the Beloved; with you I am well pleased."
>
> Luke 3:21-22

Notice that it was while Jesus was at prayer that the Holy Spirit descended upon him. It wasn't through the baptism of John. That is why Jesus assures us that when we ask our heavenly Father for the Holy Spirit to come upon us, we will always receive the Spirit. We can hear the confidence in Jesus' heart when he says: "how much more will the heavenly Father give the Holy Spirit to those who ask him"! Jesus knows that it is only in and through the Holy Spirit that we can preach the Gospel. He said to his disciples just before he ascended to heaven:

> You will receive power when the Holy Spirit has come upon you, and you will be my witnesses in Jerusalem, in all Judea and Samaria, and to the ends of the earth.
>
> Acts 1:8

Prayer is the secret of successful evangelisation, the key that opens the treasures of heaven. Jesus shows us this by his example. He never made a big decision without turning to God his Father in prayer. Sometimes he spends the full night in prayer. Before Jesus made his great decision of choosing his Twelve Apostles, he spent the whole night in prayer, asking God his Father for guidance.

As missionary disciples we often have to make serious decisions about our mission, about our parish and about how to engage in new missionary initiatives. Jesus says to us before each big decision, "learn from me". He never made a decision without giving good time to prayer. If we are engaged in any form of preaching the Gospel we have to take our cue from him. If Jesus felt it necessary to spend hours in prayer before big decisions, we too need to integrate good prayer time into every missionary activity we are engaged in. It should never be a question of getting the work done and praying when we have the time or the inclination. If we work in that way we will quickly discover that we have less and less time and less and less inclination. We should see our time in prayer as our first act of evangelising because prayer alone evangelises our hearts.

Jesus' prayer of joy

Jesus not only taught his disciples the Good News but he also sent them out to proclaim it. It was as if he said to them, "You have heard what I have been teaching you, now you go and teach others." St Luke tells us:

> After this the Lord appointed seventy others and sent them on ahead of him in pairs to every town and place where he himself intended to go. He said to them, "The harvest is plentiful, but the labourers are few; therefore ask the Lord of the harvest to send out labourers into his harvest."
>
> Luke 10:1-3

Those disciples set off on their first missionary journey and they began to experience for themselves the power of preaching in the name of Jesus. They had great reports for Jesus on their return. St Luke says, "The seventy returned with joy, saying, 'Lord, in your name even the demons submit to us'" (Luke 10:17). They had been witnessing to Christ and they experienced that by using the very name Jesus, Christ had been with them. He was present in their preaching. That is why the devils submitted to them. But Jesus said to them, "Do not rejoice at this, that the spirits submit to you, but rejoice that your names are written in heaven (Luke 10:20).

Jesus himself was filled with joy as those disciples reported all their experience of preaching in his name to him. St Luke writes:

> At that same hour Jesus rejoiced in the Holy Spirit and said, "I thank you, Father, Lord of heaven and earth, because you have hidden these things from the wise and the intelligent and have revealed them to infants; yes, Father, for such was your gracious will. All things have been handed over to me by my Father; and no one knows who the Son is except the Father, or who the Father is except the Son and anyone to whom the Son chooses to reveal him."
>
> Luke 10:21-22

We can hear the joy of Jesus in that prayer of blessing, acknowledging that the Father was indeed revealing the great mystery of our salvation to infants. He had, of course, warned us: "Truly I tell you, unless you change and become like children, you will never enter the kingdom of heaven" (Matthew 18:3). Now his disciples were entering the kingdom of heaven because, like children, they were putting all their trust in him. That was the source of their joy and the source of Jesus' joy. As Pope Francis wrote:

> The joy of the Gospel fills the hearts and lives of all who encounter Jesus. Those who accept his offer of salvation are set free from sin, sorrow, inner emptiness and loneliness.[70]

When we experience that joy of the Gospel we respond in prayer as Jesus did and say, "we bless you Father, Lord of heaven and of earth, for hiding these things from the learned and the clever and revealing them to little children", that is, revealing them to us today.

---

70 *Evangelii Gaudium*, 1.

Transfiguration as Jesus prays

While Jesus was at prayer on the mountain, Peter, James and John witnessed a visible manifestation of the truth about Jesus that Peter had professed, namely, that he is "the Christ, the Son of the living God". St Luke describes it in this way:

> Now about eight days after these sayings Jesus took with him Peter and John and James, and went up on the mountain to pray. And while he was praying, the appearance of his face changed, and his clothes became dazzling white. Suddenly they saw two men, Moses and Elijah, talking to him. They appeared in glory and were speaking of his departure, which he was about to accomplish at Jerusalem... A cloud came and overshadowed them; and they were terrified as they entered the cloud. Then from the cloud came a voice that said, "This is my Son, my Chosen; listen to him!"
>
> Luke 9:28-31. 34-35

The transfiguration of Jesus on the mountain is a prayer event. This great manifestation of the glory of Christ takes place as Jesus is in communion with his Father. Moses and Elijah come to talk to Jesus about the departure he was to accomplish in Jerusalem. "His departure" literally means "his exodus", a word that connects Jesus' approaching passion and death with that first Exodus of God's people when Moses, who is now talking to Jesus on the mountain, led them from slavery in Egypt into freedom. The death of Jesus will be the "second exodus" of God's people, not into an earthly kingdom, but into the kingdom of God. The salvation symbolised by the first exodus is about to be realised in Jesus' Exodus from this world to the glory of the Father. Moses and the great prophet Elijah are talking to Jesus about his approaching passion and death. Pope Benedict XVI wrote:

> Their topic of conversation is the Cross, but understood in the inclusive sense of Jesus' Exodus, which had to take

place in Jerusalem. Jesus' Cross is an Exodus: a departure from this life, a passage through the "Red Sea" of the Passion and a transition into glory – glory, however, that forever bears the mark of Jesus' wounds.[71]

Witnessing the transfiguration of Jesus on the mountain was a most profound experience for the three disciples. It is first and foremost an experience of what happens when Jesus prays. Because this mystery of the transfiguration is an experience of Jesus at prayer, it can become for us also a great "prayer event" as we behold in our meditation the glory of God shining on the face of Jesus. Peter could never forget it. In his second letter to the Churches he wrote:

> For he received honour and glory from God the Father when a voice was conveyed to him by the Majestic Glory, saying: "This is my Son, my Beloved; with whom I am well pleased." We ourselves heard this voice come from heaven, while we were with him on the holy mountain.
>
> 2 Peter 1:17-18

St Paul, the greatest evangelist, shares the secret of his indefatigable energy as a missionary disciple with us when he wrote: "Pray in the Spirit at all times in every prayer and supplication" (Ephesians 6:18). Prayer should never be absent from any of our evangelising enterprises. We not only pray before we go out to do the work but, as we meet people and talk with them, we try to remember that it is to Jesus that we are also speaking. Jesus totally identifies himself with each person. So, in every person we meet we can find Jesus. St Paul, before his conversion discovered this in a blinding flash. He was a persecutor of the early Church in Jerusalem and he had been authorised by the chief priests to go to Damascus and arrest any Christians he could find there. He encountered Christ on the way. St Luke writes:

---

71 *Jesus of Nazareth*, 311.

> Now as he was going along and approaching Damascus, suddenly a light from heaven flashed around him. He fell to the ground and heard a voice saying to him, "Saul, Saul, why do you persecute me?" He asked, "Who are you, Lord?" The reply came, "I am Jesus, whom you are persecuting. But get up and enter the city, and you will be told what you are to do."
>
> Acts 9:3-6

Christ's union with each human being

Jesus' personal union with those whom he had come to redeem, his identification with each one of us, made a transforming impression on Paul. We owe the wonderful truth that we are Christ's body in the world, that Christ is the head and we are the members of his body, to the revelation that Paul received from Christ on the road to Damascus. In all his letters to the churches, St Paul reminds them that they are members of Christ's body. Writing to the church in Corinth he uses the human body as an analogy:

> For just as the body is one and has many members, and all the members of the body, though many, are one body, so it is with Christ. For in the one Spirit we were all baptised into one body – Jews or Greeks, slaves or free – and we were all made to drink of one Spirit. Indeed, the body does not consist of one member but of many.
>
> 1 Corinthians 12:12-14

Because Christians "are all baptised into one body" in "the one Spirit", St Paul constantly urges them to preserve that unity:

> [Make] every effort to maintain the unity of the Spirit in the bond of peace. There is one body and one Spirit, just as you were called to the one hope of your calling, one Lord, one faith, one baptism, one God and Father of all, who is above all and through all and in all.
>
> Ephesians 4:3-6

God had revealed these great truths to Paul. Christ is so united with each brother and sister that his persecution of one of them was a persecution of Christ. That revelation of how Christ is one with his brothers and sisters totally changed Paul's life. It has the power to change our lives also, change the way we relate to one another in every circumstance. And Christ is united not just with the baptised Christians but with every single person in history. The Second Vatican Council gave us this beautiful teaching: "By his incarnation, he, the Son of God, has in a certain way united himself with each individual".[72] Jesus Christ is a brother to every single human being ever born into this world. For this reason the Vatican Council could say:

> For since Christ died for everyone, and since all are in fact called to one and the same destiny, which is divine, we must hold that the Holy Spirit offers to all the possibility of being made partakers, in a way known to God, in the paschal mystery.[73]

This very consoling teaching of the Church gives us great confidence as we go about our missionary tasks. People's salvation does not depend on us. Christ has redeemed them. But the knowledge and the joy of knowing their Redeemer does, to a certain extent, depend on us. We have good news for them, good news that St Paul summarised in one phrase "[Our Lord] was handed over to death for our trespasses and was raised to life for our justification" (Romans 4:25). That is the good news that Jesus sends us out to proclaim when he says, just before he ascended to heaven: "Go into all the world and proclaim the Good News to all creation" (Mark 16:15).

As we come to the end of this chapter on preparing our hearts and minds for the work of evangelisation, we return to the invitation we receive from Jesus when he says: "Learn from me, for I am gentle and humble in heart" (Matthew 11:29). Our best preparation for the

---

72 *Gaudium et Spes*, 22.
73 *Gaudium et Spes*, 24.

work of evangelisation, as missionary disciples, is to begin learning those lessons of gentleness and humility from Jesus. When you can approach people with those attitudes and with trust and confidence in the Holy Spirit you have graduated from the Christ's school of evangelisation. You are qualified to be his witness.

Personal spiritual exercise for internalising the message of this chapter

- Find a quiet place as free of interruptions and disruptions as possible. Centre yourself; sitting upright; breathing rhythmically; clearing your mind of all preoccupations.

- As you cross the threshold of stillness, you have come into God's presence.

- In your heart entrust yourself, with all your joys and troubles, with all your good works and sinful weaknesses, to Christ our Saviour.

- Thank Jesus for calling you to be his missionary disciple and for inviting with the words, "Learn from me, for I am gentle and humble in heart".

- As you say "Lord teach me how to be your disciple" relax and listen to what he says to you.

- Focus again on your breathing as you relax in God's presence.

- Now bring yourself gently back to continue your daily routine.

This spiritual exercise, relaxing in God's presence, will help you to personalise your understanding of becoming Christ's disciple and learning from him.

— Chapter 5 —

Preparing the parish for the work of the new evangelisation

Each new generation of men and women has to be evangelised. While they may inherit religious practices from their families or parishes, they don't inherit the gift of faith. Only God can give that gift. It comes from hearing the word of God; from opening one's heart to Jesus and accepting him as one's Lord and Saviour. It is quite possible, as I mentioned in the last chapter, for a person to know the answers to all the questions about their religion without knowing Jesus Christ. We cannot equate religious practices or religious knowledge with the faith by which we believe in Jesus Christ, with that gift and light of faith which enables us to say, "Yes, Lord, I believe that you are the Christ the Son of the living God."

It has often been said that the Church is never more than one generation away from extinction. This should not be considered a prophesy of doom. It is a simple statement of fact and has been so throughout the past two thousand years of the Church's history. If each new generation is not evangelised they will not come to faith in Jesus Christ and without that faith there would be no Church. But our faith in Christ assures us that the Church doesn't ultimately depend on us finding the right way to evangelise the next generation; it depends on Christ's promise to us that "I am with you always, to the end of the age" (Matthew 28:20). Christ will not desert his Church. The history of the Church bears witness to Christ's fidelity to his promise. The Catholic Church has lived through great persecutions in the past and has always emerged purified. The Church in Russia went through seventy years of persecution during Communist domination when Russia was officially an atheistic empire. Religious education was banned from schools. Yet, despite every effort being made to obliterate all traces of religion, the Communist regime has now disappeared and the Church has re-emerged purified. Evangelisation continued secretly in Russia, and Russian grandmothers kept the faith alive. They refused to obey their Soviet Communist rulers, and shared their faith with their grandchildren. Grandmothers are highly revered in Russia. No KGB man or policeman would interfere with the Russian babushkas. Mothers had to go out to work in the factories and the fields while grandmothers looked after the children and shared with them their Christian faith. God's regiment of faithful grandmothers had evangelised their generation of grandchildren. When the state universities, colleges and schools were closed to God, Russian children discovered the name of Jesus on the lips, and the love of Jesus in the hearts of their grandmothers. They were evangelised in their hearts.

Why a new evangelisation?

St John Paul II first used the term "a new evangelisation" in an address to Latin American Bishops in Haiti in 1983. He described what would be new about this evangelisation with these words: "new in ardour, new in methods, and new in its expressions". John Paul was very aware that profound changes were happening in human society. The Second Vatican Council, at which he was an active participant, drew attention to these changes:

> Ours is a new age of history with profound and rapid changes spreading gradually to all corners of the earth. They are the products of people's intelligence and creative activity, but they recoil upon them, upon their judgements and desires, both individual and collective, upon their ways of thinking and acting in regard to people and things, we are entitled then to speak of a real social and cultural transformation whose repercussions are felt at the religious level also.[74]

---

74 *Gaudium et Spes*, 4.

That cultural transformation – some would say revolution – was just beginning in the 1960s. Today, fifty years later, we are very aware of how our society and our culture have changed. Our Church has changed too; not as much as some people would like, and too much for others, but it is, nevertheless, changing. A very significant and heartening change is the increasing number of laypeople who now accept their vocation as missionary disciples and are eager to make the Christ they love and follow known to others. This gave great encouragement to St John Paul II. For him, it was one of the great signs of the times. He wrote:

> The commitment of the laity to the work of evangelisation is changing ecclesial life, while particular Churches are more willing to meet with members of other Christian Churches and other religions, and to enter into dialogue and cooperation with them. Above all there is a new awareness that *missionary activity is a matter for all Christians,* for all dioceses and for all parishes.[75]

That is surely the most significant change that has taken place in our Church for centuries. For many centuries, as we saw in the first chapter of this book, evangelisation was seen as the special vocation of priests and religious, especially those who went to Africa, Asia, Australia, and the Americas. They went "on the missions". Now the lay faithful in many parts of the Church are consciously assuming their vocation as missionary disciples and bringing the Good News to others. This is a providential awakening of the missionary spirit in the hearts of very many laymen and laywomen throughout the Church. As St John Paul II said, "it is changing ecclesial life", that is church life, and it will change it where it will have the greatest effect, namely, in the parish community. Has it begun to change your parish yet? Maybe you and a few friends have to make the first move!

---

75 *Redemptoris Missio,* 2.

The parish: place of encounter

It is in the parish community that people encounter the Church of Christ: they meet faithful Catholics; they get to know them; they observe them; they acquire a sense of what their religion means to them. The small local community, gathering in the name of Jesus, shines the light of faith on all comers. Jesus said to his disciples:

> You are the light of the world. A city built on a hill cannot be hidden. No one after lighting a lamp puts it under a bushel basket, but on the lampstand, and it gives light to all in the house. In the same way, let your light shine before others, so that they may see your good works and give glory to your Father in heaven.
>
> Matthew 5:14-16

The first missionary witness is given through the light that the parish lets shine. As Pope Francis says:

> The parish is the presence of the Church in a given territory, an environment for hearing God's word, for growth in the Christian life, for dialogue, proclamation, charitable outreach, worship and celebration. In all its activities the parish encourages and trains its members to be evangelisers. It is a community of communities, a sanctuary where the thirsty come to drink in the midst of their journey and a centre of constant missionary outreach.[76]

When we think about the new evangelisation, about how we should be evangelising today, the first thing we have to consider is the quality of our own parish life. Is my parish "a community of communities", a community of missionary disciples? In his great commissioning of his first disciples Jesus said, "All authority in heaven and on earth has been given to me. Go, therefore, make disciples of all

---

76 *Evangelii Gaudium*, 28.

nations" (Matthew 28:18-19). There is a vast difference between making disciples and making churchgoers. The new evangelisation is urgently needed because many people are churchgoers but they are not yet disciples. In the second chapter we saw Fr James Mallon's description of what it means to be a disciple.

To be a disciple means to become a lifelong learner. Those who haven't so far taken that step in faith will find it hard to respond to the commission that Jesus gives us to make disciples. That is why the work of evangelising has to take place within the parish community. And, as Pope Francis said above, "In all its activities the parish encourages and trains its members to be evangelisers." The parish is a community of disciples and at the same time a community of those who are not yet disciples but who are seeking a deeper relationship with the Lord Jesus.

A great diversities of parish ministries

I mentioned in chapter 2 how during a parish mission I always have a Saturday morning gathering of parishioners to evaluate the mission experience and reflect on the question: *How is our parish evangelising the neighbourhood?* Some participants in this session are always amazed when they discover that many small groups of committed parishioners are involved in a great variety of ministries to help others in the parish or city: St Vincent de Paul groups, ecumenical groups, choirs, groups supporting asylum seekers, refugees and homeless people, as well as prayer groups, marriage encounter groups, and many other outreach groups. Invariably the request is made that the list of all these groups working within the parish should be published on a noticeboard. This convinced me that parishes already have many dedicated missionary disciples able and willing to meet the apostolic challenges of our time. I feel certain that once they are invited and encouraged to face the challenge of the new evangelisation there will be a most encouraging response.

An oasis of mercy

The parish community that begins to take evangelising seriously looks first at how it reflects the face of Christ to all its members and to everyone in its neighbourhood. Everyone who enters your parish community should encounter the mercy of God incarnate in the members of the community. As we saw in chapter 1, Pope Francis uses the image of an oasis to speak about the Church and the parish. In the desert there are no rivers or lakes. But the weary travellers often come across a fertile spot where they find refreshing water: an oasis. For many travellers through the desert, an oasis was a lifesaver. Your parish is called to be an "oasis of mercy" where weary travellers, who may have lost their way in life, will find a warm and secure welcome.

We must be aware of the fact that many faithful parishioners need to find that "oasis of mercy" in their own parish community. People can be going through times of turmoil that we know nothing about. They may manifest this turmoil in the way they behave. Instead of criticising them, finding fault with them, and gossiping about them to others, we should humbly pray for them and try to be a merciful and accepting presence to them. That would be "letting one's light shine", taking the first evangelising step. Nothing has to be said. Just a smile or a "Good morning", or some outward sign of respect and regard is all that is necessary. Interestingly, one of the definitions of oasis given in the *Oxford English Dictionary* is, "an area or period of calm in the midst of turbulence". Practising Catholics can sometimes find themselves caught up in a turbulence. They may not have the confidence to talk about it, but they will be able to read the body language of fellow parishioners. If they are in some turbulence and enter the parish community in the church where nobody greets them, not even with a smile, they may walk out and never return. Such a parish fails Pope Francis' "oasis of mercy" test.

A parish that failed a parishioner

Some years ago while giving a parish mission in a large parish in London I met a lady who didn't find that oasis of mercy in her parish. I was visiting homes and when I knocked on her door she invited me in. She had been a practising Catholic most of her life but she had just recently stopped going to Mass. She was very angry. She said to me, "The thing that hurts me most is that I am not even missed." Those words still ring in my ears. There were five Masses in that church every weekend: the Saturday evening vigil Mass, three Masses on the Sunday morning and one on Sunday evening. Well over a thousand parishioners attended Mass each weekend. She used to be one of them. But nobody knew she was there and nobody knew she wasn't there. The irony of my visit struck me. I was trying to encourage her to come back to a community that neither knew her nor missed her! I realised that there were probably hundreds like her in that large parish. For her, at the time of turbulence in her life, she failed to find that oasis of mercy in her parish community. That parish had to ask itself this very serious question: in what sense is a parish, in which a member remains unknown and unacknowledged after Sunday Mass and never missed when she doesn't turn up, a Christian community? As Fr Mallon writes in answer to a similar question:

> Authentic community is a place where we are known and loved. It is a place where we find others to whom we are accountable and who are accountable to us. This is the heart of Christian community, of *koinonia*, the Greek word that can be translated as *"fellowship"*.[77]

It would be easy to put all the blame on the individual: she kept herself to herself, she didn't make herself known, she was a loner, and so on. But who made the effort to reach out to her? Did anybody really miss her when she dropped out? These are questions that every parish of missionary disciples has to ask themselves. She might surely have been missed in a Baptist or a Pentecostal community.

---

77 Mallon, *Divine Renovation*, 137.

Somebody would have been on the phone to her asking if they could help in any way.

Today as we try to see the parish as an evangelising community of missionary disciples, first of its own members and then of those who are not yet members, we have to ask how it could happen that nobody in the community noticed the absence of a woman who regularly attended the parish Mass or, if they did notice, they felt no duty to find out if she needed help of any kind? What does that say to us about the structures of the parish community? Do people attend Mass just as individuals concerned for themselves or a few of their friends, or do they genuinely have the good of the whole community at heart? We could ask this question of every parish community: how do we make sure that nobody slips away from our community unnoticed, unknown and not even missed? Pope Francis gives us his vision of the parish community:

> The parish is not an outdated institution; precisely because it possesses great flexibility, it can assume quite different contours depending on the openness and missionary creativity of the pastor and the community. While certainly not the only institution which evangelises, if the parish proves capable of self-renewal and constant adaptability, it continues to be "the Church living in the midst of the homes of her sons and daughters".[78] This presumes that it really is in contact with the homes and the lives of its people, and does not become a useless structure out of touch with people or a self-absorbed group made up of a chosen few.[79]

The lost sheep

The evangelising parish is in contact with all its members. It seeks to be "in contact with the homes and the lives of its people". But one man, the parish priest, cannot do that alone. Today, parishioners are

---

78   St John Paul II, *Christifideles Laici* ("Apostolic Exhortation of the Lay Faithful"), 26.
79   *Evangelii Gaudium*, 28.

more fully aware that each one of them can play an essential role in establishing and maintaining that contact. But the parish needs to encourage all its members to assume their responsibility. Over fifty years ago the Second Vatican council was calling for this full participation by the laity in the life and mission of the parish. It is worth pondering the recommendations from that great Council. Consider the implications of this recommendation:

> The lay ministry within the church communities is so necessary that without it the apostolate of pastors will frequently be unable to obtain its full effect.[80]

The good of the Church requires the full participation of each missionary disciple, each practising member of the parish community, in the life and mission of the parish. To be a practising Catholic means being a participating Catholic in the life and mission of the parish. If that participation is absent the parish priest will be powerless when faced with the many pastoral challenges facing the parish community today. Many young people disappear from the parish community and very often the parish doesn't have a young missionary disciple or, better still, a team of young missionary disciples, to go in search of them. Jesus' parable of the lost sheep speaks clearly to us today:

> Which one of you, having a hundred sheep and losing one of them, does not leave the ninety-nine in the wilderness and go after the one that is lost until he finds it? When he has found it, he lays it on his shoulders and rejoices. And when he comes home, he calls together his friends and neighbours, saying to them, "Rejoice with me, for I have found my sheep that was lost." Just so, I tell you, there will be more joy in heaven over one sinner who repents than over ninety-nine righteous people who need no repentance.
>
> Luke 15:4-7

---

80 *Apostolicam Actuositatem*, 10.

That is Christ's own vision of pastoral care. We don't wait for the "lost" to find their way back. We go in search. Young people evangelising young people, going in search of young people who drop out, should be the parish's response to the urgent pastoral challenges facing young people today. They know how to establish contact and maintain contact through social media.

In your parish who will take the initiative in calling forth and encouraging these young missionary disciples? Maybe you? Think about it, pray about it and talk to your friends about it. If the Lord is calling you to take an initiative will you be willing to respond? By talking it through with a few friends you will make a good decision.

Pope Francis, as we have seen, expects the parish to train evangelisers: "In all its activities the parish encourages and trains its members to be evangelisers."[81] Some parishes are very keen to see their communities deeply renewed in the Spirit and assuming their missionary role. Good initiatives are being taken to achieve this goal. I will mention just two, the Catholic Alpha programme and parish missions.

Alpha in a Catholic context

The Alpha programme came to Catholics from the Anglican Communion. Some thirty years ago it was developed in the Anglican parish of Holy Trinity Brompton, in London. Today it is estimated that 24 million people in 169 countries worldwide have followed this course. Alpha in a Catholic Context is a version of the programme specifically developed for Catholic parishes. At the invitation of Cardinal Basil Hume, the first Alpha conference for Catholics was held in 1996. It is now running in Catholic parishes in seventy countries. According to the Alpha website, it attracts young people who are asking the question: "Is there more to life than this?" And, of course, it is attracting thousands of people of all ages and of all faiths and none.

---

81 *Evangelii Gaudium*, 28.

As an evangelising initiative the Alpha programme has been highly recommended by many cardinals and bishops in the Catholic Church. Archbishop Rino Fisichella, President of the Pontifical Council for Promoting the New Evangelisation, said: "Alpha is without doubt a great experience of new evangelisation." Cardinal Shoenborn of Vienna, who edited the new Catholic Catechism, said:

> Alpha is for meeting Jesus. What I like in all that I have seen and heard about Alpha is the simplicity. For me, the Christian life has something to do with simplicity, friendship, closeness and joy. That's what I feel about Alpha and I think that's a sign that it works and that it's given from the Lord.

Cardinal Mark Quellet, Prefect of the Congregation for Bishops and President of the Pontifical Commission for Latin America, said:

> Alpha brings people closer and helps them to find that power which unites. The Alpha experience is not only a means through which one finds true life, but also a way to share the good news of the Living Christ.

Just one further recommendation comes from Father Raniero Cantalamessa, Preacher to the Papal Household:

> One of the advantages of Alpha is that it focuses on Kerygma. In the ancient Church, there was a clear distinction between the Kerygma and the Didache, the catechesis. The Kerygma was the starting point of faith, and the catechesis had to form the faith. But faith in itself blossoms only by hearing the Kerygma... I especially appreciate the ecumenical spirit of Alpha: there is no pressure on anybody to join a different denomination, but just to join Jesus.[82]

---

82 You will find these recommendations on the internet at alpha.org/catholic-context.

The endorsement of those great Catholic leaders in the new evangelisation assures us that Alpha provides an ideal setting for the proclamation of the kerygma,[83] the good news of what Jesus Christ has done for us. The programme is developed over eleven weeks. Each session starts with a meal, followed by a talk and then discussion in small groups. The talks explore the main truths of the Christian faith; the discussion in the small groups enable participants to share, deepen and interiorise their own understanding of these truths. This sharing builds a true community of faith among the participants and prepares them to share their faith with the whole parish community and with those who may want to join the community.

Alpha in a Catholic Context can enable a parish to develop and deepen the community of faith. This will be a great enrichment of parish life and enable the practising parish to become an evangelising parish. To delve further into this topic, I can highly recommend the book by Fr James Mallon, *Divine Renovation: bringing your parish from maintenance to mission.* [84]

Parish missions

The parish mission remains a most effective means for stirring up the faith of the whole practising parish community and calling on them to become witnesses to their faith in Jesus Christ. The purpose of the mission is to help a practising parish to become an evangelising parish. Before the parish community is ready to take this step, parishioners need to be renewed in their own faith and commitment to Jesus Christ. They need to get to know Jesus more intimately and personally as their Lord, their Saviour, their friend and brother who is always with them. Once they experience their relationship with Jesus in this personal way they will be able and willing to share their faith with others.

---

83 We will discuss the meaning of this in chapters 6 and 7.
84 Fr James Mallon, *Divine Renovation: bring your parish from maintenance to mission* (New London, CT: Twenty-Third Publications, 2014).

The parish community has to assume its responsibility for its lapsing members and for those who are in danger of lapsing. This should be one of the main goals of the new evangelisation in the parish. During parish missions I am always asked this question, "What are you doing for the young people?" and very rarely asked "What should our parish be doing for its young people?" The simple answer is, it should be training at least some of its committed young members to be evangelisers of the youth of the parish. As well as that, it should be constantly inviting the parents of the parish to become committed disciples and learn more about their faith. If parents haven't yet become disciples of Christ they will not be able or willing to inspire their young adult children to accept Jesus into their lives. But for many parents to take the first step towards committing as disciples of Jesus Christ, they need the love, support, encouragement, esteem and acceptance of all the committed members of their parish. That is why parish missions and evangelising programmes are so necessary for protecting the faith of the practising Catholics; for helping the practising Catholics to reach out to the lapsed members of the community; for giving young people the opportunity to think again about the meaning and purpose of their lives; for inviting people who have not yet received the gift of faith to begin to explore the meaning of the Catholic faith in Jesus Christ.[85] By feeding the practising members of the parish with the word of God, through kerygmatic peaching and good evangelistic programmes, the parish will grow and become a joyful evangelising parish.

Personal contact
Maintaining some form of personal contact with the members of the parish is even more crucial today, especially as many members live alone. This contact can only be maintained by the commitment of scores of laymen and laywomen. They will manifest Christ's love and concern for each member of the parish, whether they attend Sunday

---

85   If you feel called to become involved in the new evangelisation, speak to your parish priest and consult the website of your diocese. If you do not use the internet, ask a friend to do it for you. Dioceses have good resources for helping evangelising groups to learn more about their faith.

Mass or not. It is, in many ways, a daunting task to undertake, but once a group of the parish's missionary disciples begin reaching out in this way to keep in contact with fellow parishioners, they discover the joy of evangelising. As Pope Francis says:

> Life grows by being given away, and it weakens in isolation and comfort. Indeed those who enjoy life most are those who leave security on the shore and become excited by the mission of communicating life to others. When the Church summons Christians to take up the task of evangelisation, she is simply pointing to the source of authentic personal fulfilment. For here we discover a profound law of reality: that life is attained and matures in the measure that it is offered up in order to give life to others. This is certainly what mission means.[86]

Keeping in contact with all the members of the parish is an evangelising action because it brings to others the good news of God's love and concern for each member of the parish. In this way the whole parish community becomes the oasis of mercy for all its members. The parish which is responding to the Church's call for the new evangelisation will provide encouragement and training for their missionary disciples who go out in its name to keep in touch with all the members of the parish.

The Second Vatican Council not only strongly recommended the full participation of the laymen and laywomen in the mission of the Church but it also expressly emphasised the need for the parish community to hold general discussions on the problems facing the Church and the parish:

> The laity should develop the habit of working in the parish in close cooperation with their priests, bringing before the Church community their own problems, world problems,

---

86 *Evangelii Gaudium*, 10.

and questions regarding humanity's salvation, to examine them together and solve them by general discussion. According to their abilities the laity ought to cooperate in all the apostolic and missionary enterprises of their ecclesial family.[87]

These recommendations of the council are beginning to be embodied in parish life in a growing number of dioceses and parishes with good results. Sadly, in some places, progress has been very slow. When the parish seeks to solve problems together, through sincere dialogue, the Holy Spirit is present and will lead the community to a good solution: everyone will have a voice, know that they have been heard, and even if their particular proposal was not accepted, it was heard with respect. As the parish community develops this practice of sincere dialogue it becomes more open to the Holy Spirit and better prepared for the mission of the new evangelisation. This openness of the laity to the Holy Spirit gave St John Paul II the confidence to say in his great encyclical on the Mission of the Redeemer:

> God is opening before the Church the horizons of a humanity more fully prepared for the sowing of the Gospel. I sense that the moment has come to commit all of the Church's energies to a new evangelisation and to the mission *ad gentes*. No believer in Christ, no institution of the Church can avoid this supreme duty: to proclaim Christ to all peoples.[88]

St John Paul II preached the Gospel in 129 countries during his twenty-seven-year papacy and he saw at first-hand the urgent need "to commit all the energies of the Church to the new evangelisation". He shared with St Paul VI the deep conviction that: "Evangelising is in fact the grace and vocation proper to the Church, her deepest identity. She exists to evangelise".[89]

---

87 *Evangelii Gaudium*, 10.
88 *Redemptoris Missio*, 3.
89 *Evangelii Nuntiandi*, 14.

A Church that ceases to evangelise is no longer the Church of Christ. St John Paul II also wrote:

> No Christian community is faithful to its duty unless it is missionary: either it is a Missionary community or it is not even a Christian community, because these are simply two dimensions of the same reality, which is brought about by baptism and the other sacraments.[90]

Your parish could spend a very profitable time discussing this vision of St John Paul II. If you have to conclude that it is not yet a missionary community then you have to face the reality that, in John Paul's view, the parish is not yet a Christian community. This would be the kind of discussion that the Second Vatican Council had in mind fifty years ago when it encouraged parishes "to examine problems together and solve them by general discussion". If the missionary disciples in your parish meet together with the parish priest in this spirit of the Second Vatican Council, pray together for the enlightenment of the Holy Spirit, and discuss maturely the pastoral challenges facing the parish, they will be led by the Spirit to take good pastoral initiatives. It is the parish that never meets to discuss the pastoral challenges such as the widespread lapsing, not only of the youth but also of their parents and often their grandparents, that will suffer from low morale, and lose many of its members. The parish that is seeking to respond to all these challenges will be filled with apostolic enthusiasm and will experience a new spring in the life of the community.

Prayerful discernment of God's will for the parish
In everything concerning Christ's mission in the world today the Church is not guided by the "wisdom of the world" in her pastoral initiatives but by the discernment of spirits which is, as St Paul says, one of "the gifts of the Spirit" (see 1 Corinthians 12:1-12). Sometimes this can cause tension within a parish group as it seeks to plan a way ahead for the parish. The Church is not a business

---

90 St John Paul II, Message to World Mission Day, 20 October 1991.

corporation, guided by some strategic business models. The Church is a divine mystery, the Body of Christ in this world, guided by the Holy Spirit. Each member of the Church has immediate access to the Holy Spirit through prayer, humility of heart and a willingness to listen respectfully and attentively to what others are saying. In discerning a way forward for the parish or community we have to give up classifying people as conservative or liberals, right wing or left wing. As St Paul said:

> You have stripped off your old behaviour with your old self, and you have put on a new self which will progress towards true knowledge the more it is renewed in the image of its Creator; and in that image there is no room for distinction between Greek or Jew... or between barbarian and Scythian, slave and free. There is only Christ: he is everything and he is in everything.
>
> Colossians 3:9-11

Prayerful discernment in a parish or community gathering is the way "to progress towards true knowledge". We don't turn up to a parish pastoral meeting convinced that we know the best way forward. We come to discern what the Holy Spirit is saying to the parish today. The first business of any such gathering should always be turning to God in prayer. We ask God to guide us. We may know a step of the missionary journey that we want the parish to take, but we cannot be certain that this step should be the first step. What you are proposing may be the right step when the parish has moved forward a few steps on its apostolic journey.

Prayerful discernment enables us to peacefully accept when the Spirit seems to be indicating that a different first step should be taken. The big enemy of pastoral creativity and initiatives, as Pope Francis often says, is "immobility" or "rigidity". The fact that nothing has changed in the past twenty or thirty years is not a sign of being guided by the Spirit. The parish that is willing to take a new missionary initiative, even if some members think it will fail, shows the signs of being led by the Spirit. Jesus said to his disciples two thousand years ago, "Go and make disciples of all nations" (Matthew 28:19). That is the kind of initiative that the Lord takes. When those disciples were filled with the Holy Spirit at Pentecost they set out to evangelise the whole world. Guided and empowered by the Holy Spirit, those men and women, most of them uneducated, went forth in confidence and began the great missionary work of making disciples of all nations, a task that, from a purely human point of view, was impossible. But it was not impossible for God. We have to have that same confidence as we embark on the work of the new evangelisation in our parishes today. The Holy Spirit still guides Christ's missionary disciples. As we go forth within our parishes and neighbourhoods to bring the Good News to others, the Holy Spirit will empower us, teach us how to proceed, and guide our steps.

Living with disagreements
The fact that some members of the parish may object very strongly to what is being undertaken or want nothing to do with it is no reason for marginalising them. We should simply encourage them to pray for the parish to do God's will. The parish exists to bring the Good News of Christ to others. There may be a disagreement about the best way of evangelising but this disagreement, within a discerning community, never leads to ill will, rejection, or treating others as obstacles.

If an individual member or a few members of the parish don't yet have the confidence to engage in any kind of evangelising outreach, they should be encouraged to exercise their ministry of prayer for the parish. While others commit to engaging in some work of evangelisation, they can commit to supporting the whole parish in prayer. If a parish has exposition of the Blessed Sacrament they could be encouraged to devote one hour of adoration each week for the evangelising teams in the parish. Their time of adoration would be a major contribution to the evangelising witness of the parish.

A school of evangelisation

The parish community's dialogue about how to enhance the missionary dimension of parish activities is, in itself, a school of evangelisation where the parishioners learn how to hone their skills of communication. We keep in mind the words that St Paul wrote: "Let your speech always be gracious, seasoned with salt, so that you may know how you ought to answer everyone" (Colossians 4:5). The joy of the Gospel should be audible in the way we relate and speak to everyone. It should set the tone for any community dialogue, especially about bringing the Good News to others. St Peter gives us this lesson: "In your hearts sanctify Christ as Lord. Always be ready to make your defence to anyone who demands from you an account of the hope that is in you; yet do it with gentleness and reverence" (1 Peter 3:15-16). Those are key words for forming within ourselves the right attitude towards everyone, especially towards those who may be seeking a deeper meaning in life but who may be hostile to our Catholic faith. We have to train ourselves to respond to everyone, friend or foe alike, with courtesy and respect and with "salt", or wit. In an animated parish community meeting, where there will be many points of view about how the whole parish could become an evangelising parish, there will be plenty of opportunities for exercising these virtues.

Listening to the Holy Spirit

The parish meeting to discern how the parish could become an evangelising parish is not a debating society where someone has to win the debate by clever arguments. It is a time for listening, not just to what others are saying, but most of all to what the Holy Spirit is saying to the community. It is God's will for the parish that the meeting is seeking to discern. The second petition in the Lord's Prayer guides the hearts of all those present: "Thy will be done on earth". In the parish discerning process, the community is really praying, thy will be done in our parish. Each participant who is truly seeking God's will says to God, in the words of Jesus in the garden of Gethsemane, "not my will but yours be done" (Luke 22:42). We have to be willing to surrender our own will, let go of our own plans. When God manifests his will through the respectful exchange of views, those who are truly seeking to know the divine will experience inner peace and can wholeheartedly accept it, even though they may have been arguing for a different course of action.

The individuals who may be excessively set on getting their own way are not really involved in the discernment process. Unconsciously, it is their own will, not God's will, that they want done. They may not be able, at that moment, to accept the community's discernment. But that doesn't mean that they have become outsiders. The community will continue to relate to them as brothers and sisters and show them the respect, compassion and sensitivity which are the hallmark of how Christians relate to everyone. The parish that can relate to all its members with respect, compassion and sensitivity is now well prepared to begin evangelising the neighbourhood or the city. That is why we can say that the parish is a "school of evangelisation".

Respect

Every human being, made in the image and likeness of God and redeemed by Jesus Christ, is our brother or sister. We love them as Jesus asked us to do when he said, "love one another just as I have loved you" (John 15:12). If they have become our enemies, we still love them because Jesus says, "Love your enemies and pray for those who persecute you" (Matthew 5:44). Our manifestation of this love is shown through the respect we have in our hearts for each person. Sometimes I have heard a person boast that people have to earn his respect. That is an unchristian attitude to cultivate.

Jesus showed great respect to groups of people who were marginalised in his society because they had been expelled from the synagogues and despised as "tax collectors and sinners". A self-respecting Pharisee would have nothing to do with them. But

Jesus even called one of them to be his disciple. St Luke writes: "After this he went out and saw a tax-collector named Levi, sitting at the tax booth, and he said to him, 'Follow me'. And he got up, left everything, and followed him" (Luke 5:27-28). A man who would have been regarded as a scoundrel and a thief has now joined the intimate circle of Jesus' disciples.[91] That would have raised a few eyebrows. But then, to make matters worse, Levi, wanting to celebrate the new life that Jesus had given him as his disciple, invited his friends to a celebration dinner in his house. St Luke continues, "Levi gave a great banquet for him in his house, and there was a large crowd of tax-collectors and others sitting at the table with them" (Luke 5:29). Not everyone, however, was celebrating Levi's new life. As St Luke says, "The Pharisees and their scribes were complaining to his disciples, saying, 'Why do you eat and drink with tax-collectors and sinners?'" (Luke 5:30). They were shocked and disgusted that Jesus' who could heal the sick and cast out evil spirits, should be sitting at table with such a rabble. Jesus responded to their complaints and said, "Those who are well have no need of a physician, but those who are sick; I have come to call not the righteous but sinners to repentance" (Luke 5:31-32).

Compassion
Jesus invites us to be like the heavenly Father in the way we show compassion: "Be merciful, just as your Father is merciful" (Luke 6:36). Jesus himself was full of mercy and compassion for everyone he met, especially those who were poor and marginalised. A parish community cannot withhold compassion from anyone, and certainly not from those members who don't want to get involved in the parish programmes for evangelising. The sure sign that the parish community is ready for the new evangelisation is their peaceful spirit in discussing serious pastoral issues, where disagreements

---

91 Tax collectors in Israel at the time of Jesus collected the taxes for the Roman Emperor. They had a fixed sum of money to collect. But many of them cheated the people by extorting more than was required and keeping the extra cash for themselves. The tax collector Zacchaeus in his confession to the Lord mentioned his past dishonesty (Luke 19:8). There is no reason to believe that Levi was dishonest even if in the popular estimation all tax collectors were cheats.

are inevitable, but where the bonds of love and peace remain intact. Your parish is experiencing what St Paul said:

> In him you also, when you had heard the word of truth, the Gospel of your salvation, and had believed in him, were marked with the seal of the promised Holy Spirit; this is the pledge of our inheritance towards redemption as God's own people, to the praise of his glory.
>
> Ephesians 1:13-14

Because St Paul saw the community of the faithful as the Body of Christ, he was always most concerned that the peace of Christ would radiate the whole body. Pope Francis regularly returns to this theme in his homilies and letters:

> Here and now, especially where we are a "little flock" (Luke 1:32), the Lord's disciples are called to live as a community which is the salt of the earth and the light of the world (Matthew 5:13-16). We are called to bear witness to a constantly new way of living together in fidelity to the Gospel. Let us not allow ourselves to be robbed of community.[92]

Very often people who disrupt parish community meetings are in inner pain, not visible on the surface, but manifested in their disruptive interventions at meetings. We have to relate to them, not just by disagreeing with what they are saying, but by showing them compassion. The very word compassion means to "suffer with". Instead of trying to persuade them that they are wrong or obstructive, we show them compassion and try to leave them feeling and knowing that they are valuable and necessary members of the community. We should always give them the gift of time. They may not be ready to respond positively today but that doesn't mean they will not be ready at some future date to respond positively and often creatively. The community's compassion is a revelation of God's

92 *Evangelii Gaudium*, 92.

love for them and it heals their wounds. As the community grows in this compassion for all its members it is being well prepared by the Holy Spirit to begin a confident evangelising outreach to others.

Sensitivity

Sensitivity to the feelings of others is the manifestation of true Christian love and understanding. Sensitivity is the soul of empathy. Today we place great store on empathy. We can define empathy as the ability to know how a person is feeling and why he or she is feeling that way and then being able to communicate to them, non-verbally through our body language, that we understand. If we don't train ourselves as a community to be attentive to how others are feeling we are in danger of walking roughshod over their feelings. Because God has created us as community people, in need of the fellowship of brothers and sisters, we must always seek to be sensitive to how others in the parish community are feeling. You will always find the "macho type" who seems to boast, "I don't care how you are feeling, I am going to tell you the truth". Such an attitude distorts the truth. Our first duty is to love the person and then, having sensitively established a relationship, we may be able to speak the truth. In his homily for the canonisation of St Edith Stein, the great Jewish convert and philosopher who became a Carmelite nun and was killed in the Nazi death camp of Auschwitz during the Second World War, St John Paul II quoted her famous remark: "Do not accept anything as the truth if it lacks love. And do not accept anything as love if it lacks truth. One without the other becomes a destructive lie".[93]

Sensitivity is key to evangelising. The more the parish community prizes and cultivates sensitivity to the feelings of its members, the more ready the members become to undertake the work of evangelising. They will be well prepared to relate to others sensitively as they bring the Gospel of Christ to them. Pope Francis is so certain of this that he keeps repeating: "It is not by proselytizing

---

93 St John Paul II, homily for the canonisation of Edith Stein, 11 October 1998.

that the Church grows, but by attraction".[94] The parish community that cultivates that triad of *respect, compassion and sensitivity*[95] for its own members will attract others who will want to know "the reason for the hope that you have" (1 Peter 3:15). It will become an evangelising parish.

---

94 *Evangelii Gaudium*, 14.

95 Fr James Martin SJ's much acclaimed book, *Building A Bridge* (San Francisco: HarperCollins, 2017) is based on those three great virtues of respect, compassion and sensitivity.

Personal spiritual exercise for internalising the message of this chapter

- Find a quiet place as free of interruptions and disruptions as possible. Centre yourself; sitting upright; breathing rhythmically; clearing your mind of all preoccupations.

- As you cross the threshold of stillness, you have come into God's presence.

- In your heart entrust yourself – with all your worries and troubles, with all your good works and sinful weaknesses – to Christ our Saviour.

- Thank Jesus for your parish community and all it has done for you and your family.

- As you pray, "Lord, only you can give our parish the grace to become an evangelising parish," relax and listen to what he says to you.

- Focus again on your breathing as you relax in God's presence.

- Now bring yourself gently back to continue your daily routine.

This spiritual exercise, relaxing in God's presence, will help you to personalise the truth that, since your parish community is full of missionary disciples, the Lord wants the parish to live out its deepest identity and become an evangelising parish.

— Chapter 6 —

The proclamation of the good news of our salvation: the kerygma

Salvation is a totally gratuitous gift of God, offered to every single human born into this world, because of what our Lord Jesus Christ has done for us. We cannot earn, nor do we deserve salvation. But, as we open our hearts in faith and accept Jesus Christ as our saviour, we receive it. St Paul says:

> God our saviour... desires everyone to be saved and to come to full knowledge of the truth. For there is one God; there is also one mediator between God and humankind, Christ Jesus, himself human, who gave himself a ransom for all.
>
> 1 Timothy 2:3-6

When we think of our salvation, of our need for God, we say with St John Paul II: "The Redeemer of Man, Jesus Christ, is the centre of the universe and of history".[96] Christ is at the centre of our history and as we open our hearts in faith to receive Christ into our lives he becomes the centre of our lives also. With Christ at the centre of our lives we know who we are: we are the redeemed. Our redemption is what Jesus Christ is speaking about when he says to Nicodemus, "For God so loved the world that he gave his only Son, so that everyone who believes in him may not perish but may have eternal life" (John 3:16). That is our great proclamation of faith.

The kerygma
The proclamation of what Jesus Christ has done for us has been called, in the Greek language of the New Testament, the *kerygma*, the proclamation, the first announcing of the Gospel. It is not catechetical instruction, nor teaching about morality, but the proclamation of the death and resurrection of Jesus Christ for our salvation.

---

96 *Redemptor Hominis*, 1.

When a king or an emperor at the time of Jesus had an important message to convey to their subjects they sent a herald into the market place to ring a bell, call for attention, and deliver the message with a loud proclamation. That was a kerygma. When Christ's disciples began to deliver the most important message the world has ever heard, the message of our salvation through what Jesus Christ has done for us, they adopted that word. The proclamation of our salvation was called the kerygma. The message wasn't about what we have to do to obtain eternal life; it was about what Christ has done for us to receive the gift of eternal life. The message wasn't about morality, nor was it about the Church; it was specifically about Jesus Christ the Son of God who had been crucified, died and was buried, who rose from the dead on the third day and poured out the Holy Spirit on his disciples. This is St Peter's first proclamation of salvation after the Holy Spirit had descended on the disciples: "This Jesus God raised up, and of that all of us are witnesses. Being therefore exalted at the right hand of God, and having received from the Father the promise of the Holy Spirit, he has poured out this that you both see and hear" (Acts 2:32-33). That was the first public declaration, the *kerygmatic* proclamation of what Jesus Christ has done for us.

After St Peter had healed a man, who had been a cripple from his birth, there was great excitement among the people. But St Peter and St John were arrested and kept in prison overnight. In the morning they had to appear before the Sanhedrin, the Jewish court, in the Temple, where the chief priests began to interrogate them:

> "By what power or by what name did you do this?" Then Peter, filled with the Holy Spirit, said to them, "Rulers of the people and elders, if we are questioned today because of a good deed done to someone who was sick and are asked how this man has been healed, let it be known to all of you, and to all the people of Israel, that this man is standing before you in good health by the name of Jesus

Christ of Nazareth, whom you crucified, whom God raised from the dead. This Jesus is 'the stone that was rejected by you, the builders; it has become the cornerstone.' There is salvation in no one else, for there is no other name under heaven given among mortals by which we must be saved."

Acts 4: 7-12

St Peter gave them in a few sentences the complete summary of what Christ had done for them and for us. That is what the kerygma is: a short, clear, and simple announcement of the mystery of our redemption through Christ's death and resurrection. It is the word of God. Christ himself is present in that word.

The first duty of the evangelist is to announce the Good News of Our Lord Jesus Christ. St Paul, when he was invited by the president of the synagogue in Pisidia to speak "a word of encouragement" to those present said:

We bring you the good news that what God promised to our ancestors he has fulfilled for us, their children, by raising Jesus... Let it be known to you therefore, my brothers, that through this man forgiveness of sins is proclaimed to you; by this Jesus everyone who believes is set free from all those sins from which you could not be freed by the law of Moses.

Acts 13:32-33. 38

The kerygma, the first proclamation of our salvation, is always about Our Lord Jesus Christ and about what he has done for us.

You will find it helpful to read the following texts in the Acts of Apostles where St Peter is proclaiming the kerygma, the message of our salvation:

Acts 2:14-39; Acts 3:12-26; Acts 4:8-12; Acts 5:29-32; Acts 10:34-43

Read also these texts from Acts where St Paul proclaims the kerygma:

Acts 13:16-41; Acts 17; Acts 22-31; Acts 22; Acts 26:1-19; Acts 28:23-28

As you ponder those texts, the first proclamation of Jesus Christ as our Lord and Saviour, you will get a good sense of the meaning of the kerygma and the difference between kerygmatic preaching and other forms of preaching or teaching. Every sermon should include, in some way, the proclamation of what Jesus Christ does for us. Without the salvation which he has secured for us we would never be able to live the Christian life. That is why we must never reduce our Christian faith to a moral or ethical system.

St Paul's letters
We will look now at a few texts from the letters of St Paul. The briefest summary of the kerygma is surely this sentence:

> [We] believe in him who raised Jesus our Lord from the dead, who was handed over to death for our trespasses and was raised for our justification.
>
> Romans 4:24-25

In just one sentence Paul sums up the mystery and the work of our salvation.

Paul summarises his message again with these words:

> "The word is near you, on your lips and in your heart" (that is, the word of faith that we proclaim); because if you confess with your lips that Jesus is Lord and believe in your heart that God raised him from the dead, you will be saved.
>
> Romans 10:8-9

This is a clear, simple proclamation of how we receive salvation from Christ. Paul says in the next sentence of the passage just quoted: "For one believes with the heart and so is justified, and one confesses with the mouth and so is saved" (Romans 10:10). People could easily remember this succinct formulation of the mystery of our salvation.

In his first letter to the Church in Corinth, St Paul describes how he arrived in that great pagan city:

> I came among you in weakness, in fear and in great trembling and what I spoke and proclaimed [kerygma]was not meant to convince by philosophical argument, but to demonstrate the convincing power of the Spirit, so that your faith should depend not on human wisdom but on the power of God.
>
> 1 Corinthians 2:3-5

In his second letter to the Corinthians, St Paul tells us why he keeps returning to his fundamental vision of what Christ did for us:

> For the love of Christ urges us on, because we are convinced that one has died for all; therefore all have died. And he died for all, so that those who live might live no longer for themselves, but for him who died and was raised for them.
>
> 2 Corinthians 5:14-15

Christ died for us and he was raised to life so that we can now live with his life, his resurrected life. That is why he came, as he told us: "I came that they may have life, and have it abundantly" (John 10:10). It is through his death and resurrection that we have received that fullness of life. St Paul explained this to the Corinthians in this way:

> So if anyone is in Christ, there is a new creation: everything old has passed away; see everything has become new. All this is from God, who reconciled us to himself through Christ, and has given us the ministry of reconciliation.
>
> 2 Corinthians 5:17-18

St Paul sees in what Christ has done for us "a new creation". Our old creation, fallen through sin, has gone and we have become God's new creation, his beloved sons and daughters.

St Paul begins his letter to the Galatians with these words: "Paul an apostle – sent neither by human commission nor from human authorities, but through Jesus Christ and God the Father, who raised him from the dead" (Galatians 1:1). Whenever Paul mentions Jesus Christ he has to remind us that Jesus died for our sins and that God raised him to life for our justification so that we can become a new creation and live a new life. That is the kerygma, the great revelation and proclamation of what Christ has done for us.

Christ is present in the proclamation

This public announcement of who Jesus Christ is, and what God has done for us through him, introduces the person of Jesus to the listeners. The aim of this proclamation is to open the hearts of the hearers to faith in Jesus Christ. St John Paul II described this kerygmatic announcement in this way:

> The initial ardent proclamation by which a person is one day overwhelmed and brought to the decision to entrust himself to Jesus Christ by faith.[97]

The message of salvation

We have the message of salvation for the whole human race and we must deliver it with joy and with confidence. The announcement of who Jesus Christ is and what he has done for us is the heart of the proclamation of the Gospel. The word that proclaims what Jesus does for us through his death and resurrection is not just a human word; it also contains the word of God spoken by Jesus himself. Christ is present in that very act of preaching. Fr Paul Hitz C.Ss.R wrote in a classic text sixty years ago:

> Whatever the mode of this active presence of Christ in preaching (which cannot be called sacramental in the strict sense), one thing is certain: it is Christ the Lord himself

---

97   St John Paul II, *Catechesi Tradendae* ("Apostolic Exhortation on Catechesis in Our Time"), 25.

who, through the preaching of his apostles, speaks to men, calls them, sanctifies them, saves them. Or, if they reject him, judges and condemns them. Despite its form being so dependent on the talents and culture of the preacher, despite all the human weakness and unworthiness involved, Christian preaching effects a coming into this world of the Kingdom and salvation of God, a mysterious presence of the risen Christ and his redeeming mystery. Christian preaching is a saving event, a personal meeting between God and men, between Christ and his hearers in the power of the Holy Spirit. It puts the mystery of Christ at man's disposal, and establishes the contract whereby he is saved.[98]

Because Jesus himself is present in the proclamation of his saving death and resurrection he says to his missionary disciples, "Whoever listens to you listens to me, and whoever rejects you rejects me, and whoever rejects me rejects the one who sent me" (Luke 10:16). People today didn't walk the roads of Galilee two thousand years ago with Jesus nor listen to his great life-giving teaching, but the Lord Jesus is not in the past; he is in the present. Those who listen to the word of God proclaimed today, to that kerygma which announces the saving work of Jesus, hear the same word of salvation. The word of salvation is not just spoken by the preacher or the teacher. It is spoken by Jesus himself.

Centrality of the kerygma

Pope Francis teaches very clearly that we must never neglect nor presume that the kerygma, the proclamation of Jesus Christ as Lord and Saviour, has already been heard and assimilated. He writes:

The centrality of the kerygma calls for stressing those elements which are most needed today; it has to express

---

98   Paul Hitz C.Ss.R, *To Preach the Gospel* (New York: Sheed and Ward, 1963), 60.

God's saving love which precedes any moral and religious obligation on our part; it should not impose truth but appeal to freedom; it should be marked by joy, encouragement, liveliness and a harmonious balance which will not reduce preaching to a few doctrines which are at times more philosophical than evangelical. All this demands on the part of the evangeliser certain attitudes which foster openness to the message: approachability, readiness for dialogue, patience, a warmth and welcome which is non-judgmental.[99]

Pope Francis is re-emphasising the teaching of the bishops of Latin America and the Caribbean who published a great, magisterial document on evangelisation known as *The Aparecida Document* in 2007. At that time Pope Francis was Cardinal Archbishop of Buenos Aires in Argentina and chairman of the committee which produced the final draft of this magnificent document. The document deals extensively with the centrality of the kerygma in the process of Christian formation and preaching. It states:

Without the kerygma, the other aspects of this process are condemned to sterility, with hearts not truly converted to the Lord. Only out of the kerygma does the possibility of a true Christian initiative occur. Hence the Church should have it present in all its actions.[100]

We are becoming more aware today that without a profound Christian formation, without establishing a personal relationship, a true friendship with Jesus Christ, Catholics of all ages, but especially the young, will struggle and may even abandon the faith of their baptism. *The Aparecida Document* teaches this fundamental truth of Christian experience:

---

99 *Evangelii Gaudium*, 165.
100 *V* General Conference of the Bishops of Latin America and the Caribbean, *The Aparecida Document* (United States: Creatspace Independent Publishing Platform, 2007), 278.

The primary mission of formation is to help the members of the Church to always be with Christ, and thus to recognise, welcome, internalize, and develop the experience and values that constitute Christian identity and mission in the world... At the foundation of these dimensions is the power of the kerygmatic proclamation. People feel the contagious power of the Spirit and the Word and are led to listen to Jesus Christ, to believe in him as their Saviour, to recognise him as the one who gives full meaning to their life, and to follow in his footsteps.[101]

The challenge we are facing in our work of evangelisation today is that many people who say they don't believe in God have never heard of Jesus and many who have heard of him think he is a great historical figure in the past. They have not yet heard the good news of the resurrection of Jesus from the dead. Jesus, the liberator and Saviour, the one who alone can fill the heart with peace, is unknown to them and so they do not come to him for fullness of life. St Paul says:

> For, "Everyone who calls on the name of the Lord shall be saved." But how are they to call on one in whom they have not believed? And how are they to believe in one of whom they have never heard? And how are they to hear without someone to proclaim him? And how are they to proclaim him unless they are sent?... So faith comes from what is heard, and what is heard comes through the word of Christ.
>
> Romans 10:13-15. 17

The Church has been entrusted with "the message of salvation", the Good News of Jesus Christ who came to redeem us. Each generation of Christians has a solemn duty to make Jesus Christ known as our Saviour. Throughout the history of the Church, evangelists and

---

101 *The Aparecida Document*, 279.

teachers have done their best to make the message heard. And, in God's mysterious ways, the message was welcomed; people opened their hearts to receive the gift of faith and salvation; the Gospel has been preached to the ends of the earth. In many parts of the world the message of our salvation in Jesus Christ is being welcomed by millions of new Christians. Our biggest challenge today, and indeed our greatest sadness, is that Europe and what is called the First World that formerly embraced the Christian faith have, in large numbers, turned away from the Christian faith and no longer call "on the name of the Lord". That is why the Church is so urgently calling all of us to undertake a new evangelisation. We have to proclaim Christ afresh in our time with the full conviction that the risen Jesus himself is in our proclamation.

When the proclamation was about what we had to do

There have been times in our preaching and teaching when the focus moved from what Jesus did for us, to redeem us, and became centred on what we had to do to receive salvation. The Good News was often heard as bad news because preachers or teachers were confronting people with their sinful weakness and not really proclaiming Jesus Christ who alone can redeem us. Some preachers wrongly assumed that their Christian listeners already knew all that Jesus had done for them and now they had to press home, in their sermons, what people had to do to secure their salvation. The emphasis was more frequently on the Ten Commandments, especially the sixth and ninth commandments dealing with matters of sexuality and marriage, than on Christ's redeeming love. Morality was presented in a legalistic and moralistic way. People who didn't know Jesus Christ as their Lord and Saviour, even though they may have been churchgoers, felt crushed and defeated by their own sinfulness. This was a failure to preach the Gospel. Pope Francis encourages us to take a different approach:

> Before all else, the Gospel invites us to respond to the God of love who saves us, to see God in others and to go

forth from ourselves to seek the good of others. Under no circumstances can the invitation be obscured! All of the virtues are at the service of this response of love. If this invitation does not radiate forcefully and attractively, the edifice of the Church's moral teaching risks becoming a house of cards, and this is our greatest risk. It would mean that it is not the Gospel which is being preached, but certain doctrinal or moral points based on specifically ideological options. The message will run the risk of losing its freshness and will cease to have "the fragrance of the Gospel".[102]

A crucial dimension of evangelisation was being ignored, namely the proclamation that Jesus Christ died for our sins and rose for our justification. That means that we are not defeated by our sinful weakness. We put all our faith and trust in Christ who has redeemed us, not in our own strength, to live a virtuous life.

Baptised but not evangelised

St John Paul II was well aware that often children who have been baptised grow up in a home where there is no real religious faith. He wrote:

> Initial evangelisation has often not taken place. A certain number of children baptised in infancy come for catechesis in the parish without receiving any other initiation into faith and still without any explicit personal attachment to Jesus Christ; they only have the capacity to believe placed within them by baptism and the presence of the Holy Spirit; and opposition is quickly created by the prejudices... of the positivist spirit of their education.[103]

Those children and many adults with similar backgrounds have been baptised but not evangelised. They haven't heard the kerygma, the proclamation of what Jesus Christ has done for them. They don't

---

102 *Evangelii Gaudium.* 39.
103 *Catechesi Tradendae,* 19.

know Jesus Christ. They may know the Catechism but they haven't as yet heard the good news that Jesus Christ is their Lord and Saviour and so they haven't accepted him into their lives. They have been introduced to the doctrine and teaching of the Church but they haven't been introduced to the person of Jesus Christ. They need to encounter Jesus Christ in a personal way. It is worth quoting again the succinct summary of our Christian faith by Pope Benedict XVI:

> Being a Christian is not the result of an ethical choice or a lofty idea, but the encounter with... a person, which gives life a new horizon and a decisive direction.[104]

It is through this getting to know Christ personally that the Christian faith takes root and gives new meaning and purpose to life. Teaching the Catechism to people who have not yet met Jesus Christ, who have not accepted him as their Lord and Saviour, will give them knowledge of what the Church teaches, but it doesn't bring them into a personal relationship with Jesus Christ. This relationship comes through faith and, as St Paul says, "faith comes from what is heard, and what is heard comes through the word of Christ" (Romans 10:17). It is through hearing the kerygma that faith is born in the heart.

The Church all over the world today urgently needs to make sure that this kerygmatic proclamation is at the heart of every Christian formation programme. Programmes that remain on the intellectual level and never lead the participants into the experiential dimension, as *The Aparecida Document* said, "are condemned to sterility, with hearts not truly converted to the Lord".[105] Every Christian formation programme must give pride of place to Jesus Christ as our Lord and Saviour.

Reclaiming the message of the kerygma

We have to reclaim the simple and yet profound message of our salvation, the kerygma message, that makes it clear that we cannot

---

104 *Deus Caritas Est*, 1.
105 *The Aparecida Document*, 278.

reduce our Christian faith to a system of ethics or morality. Our faith is in what God has done for us in Christ. St Paul gives us the right approach:

> Blessed be the God and Father of our Lord Jesus Christ, who has blessed us in Christ with every spiritual blessing in the heavenly places, just as he chose us in Christ before the foundation of the world to be holy and blameless before him in love. He destined us for adoption as his children through Jesus Christ, according to the good pleasure of his will.
>
> Ephesians 1:3-5

Only in the light of God's revelation can we know the truth about ourselves and the truth about the relationship that God wants to have with us. As St Paul says, "God chose us in Christ before the world was made". That is a long time ago! God had us in mind even before he created the world for us. As we saw in the first chapter, God reveals to us how he made us and how he sees us and how much he loves us. This is the good news of our creation and of our redemption. Pope Francis wrote these uplifting words in his great encyclical *Laudato Si'* ("On Care for our Common Home"):

> The Creator can say to each one of us: "Before I formed you in the womb, I knew you" (Jeremiah 1:5). We were conceived in the heart of God, and for this reason "each of us is the result of a thought of God. Each of us is willed, each of us is loved, each of us is necessary".[106]

As human beings our dignity is immense. By creating us in his own image and likeness, God, who is love, placed in our hearts, in our innermost being, the capacity to love. It is in and through our capacity to love, as God loves, that we image God and act in the likeness of God. This love is the motivating power of our life. Everything we do is ultimately inspired by the desire to love or be loved.

---

106 Pope Francis, *Laudato Si'* ("On Care for our Common Home"), 65.

St John Paul II said:

> Humans cannot live without love. They remain a being that is incomprehensible for themselves, their lives are senseless, if love is not revealed to them, if they do not encounter love, if they do not experience it and make it their own, if they do not participate in it.[107]

Christ, in his great act of redeeming love, through his death and resurrection, has made it possible for us once again to love as he loves. We have become, as St Paul says, "a new creation" with the new capacity to love as Christ loves us.

He is risen

The great proclamation of our faith is that Jesus Christ who was crucified, died and was buried is risen from the dead. He is alive and he is with us. He has destroyed death and revealed the resurrection. As St Paul says:

> This grace was already given to us, in Christ Jesus before the ages began, but it has now been revealed through the appearing of our Saviour Christ Jesus who abolished death and brought life and immortality through the Gospel. For this Gospel I was appointed a herald and an apostle and a teacher.
>
> 2 Timothy 1:9-11

The resurrection of Jesus from the dead achieves for us the new creation of our immorality. Jesus, as St Paul said, is the "firstborn from the dead" (Colossians 1:18). We will share in Christ's resurrection. Our bodies too, with Christ, will be raised from the dead. Death was never God's plan for his people. As scripture says, "God did not make death, and he does not delight in the death of the living" (Wisdom 1:13). Death came through that original sin of our first parents. God had warned them that the day they ate of the

---

107 *Redemptor Hominis*, 10.

tree of knowledge of good and evil they would die. They ate, they died and death entered the human world.[108] Now, through the death of Christ, eternal death has been abolished. We remind ourselves of this fundamental truth during Mass when we proclaim, after the consecration: "Dying you destroyed our death, rising you restored our life, Lord Jesus come in glory". Jesus died for us so that through his death he could destroy our death. St Paul proclaimed:

> When this perishable body puts on imperishability, and this mortal body put on immortality, then the saying that is written will be fulfilled: "Death has been swallowed up in victory. Where, O death, is your victory? Where, O death, is your sting?"... Thanks be to God, who gives us the victory through our Lord Jesus Christ.
>
> 1 Corinthians 15:54-57

Jesus rose from the dead to give us immortality and eternal life. The Church prays in the Preface of the funeral Mass, "For your faithful people, Lord, life is changed, not ended". The resurrection of Jesus manifests both the destruction of that deadly poison of sin, the cause of our death, and the restoration of that eternal life which God wills us to have and to share with him for ever. Jesus says, "This is indeed the will of my Father, that all who see the Son and believe in him may have eternal life; and I will raise them up on the last day" (John 6:40). Everyone who believes in Jesus Christ the Son of God has eternal life.

When St Peter proclaimed to the citizens of Jerusalem on that first Pentecost day "let the entire house of Israel know with certainty that God has made him both Lord and Messiah, this Jesus whom you crucified" (Acts 2:36), many of them opened their hearts to receive this good news. St Luke writes:

> Now when they heard this, they were cut to the heart and said to Peter and to the other apostles, "Brothers,

---

108 Read Genesis 3 for the story of how sin and death entered the world.

what should we do?" Peter said to them, "Repent, and be baptised every one of you in the name of Jesus Christ so that your sins may be forgiven; and you will receive the gift of the Holy Spirit. For the promise is for you, for your children, and for all who are far away, everyone whom the Lord our God calls to him."

Acts 2:37-39

In his second great sermon to the people, St Peter shows the compassion of Christ as he makes allowance for all those who had clamoured for the death of Jesus:

And now, friends, I know that you acted in ignorance, as did also your rulers. In this way God fulfilled what he had foretold through all the prophets, that his Messiah would suffer. Repent therefore, and turn to God so that your sins may be wiped out.

Acts 3:17-19

Conversion

Faced with the resurrection of Jesus, our response is to "turn to God", repent of our sins, and open our hearts to receive the Holy Spirit. Jesus began his preaching of the kingdom of God with these words: "The time is fulfilled, and the kingdom of God is near; repent and believe the good news" (Mark 1:15). It is the very awareness of what Jesus Christ has done for us through his death and resurrection that moves us to repent, to change our minds about our priorities in life, and to open our hearts to Christ's great love for us. Once we turn to God, asking for mercy and forgiveness, all our sins are washed away. Sometimes people feel that their sins are too big even for God! We can assure them that although we cannot take away our own sins, Christ can and will take away all our sins because he is "the Lamb of God who takes away the sin of the world" (John 1:29). All we have to do is to believe in Christ with the gift of faith which the Holy Spirit infuses into our hearts. Then we open our hearts to Christ and ask his pardon for our sins. All our sins are forgiven and we are received into the family of God which is the Church. Christ rejects no one who turns to him for forgiveness; neither does the Church. Jesus said to the apostles when he rose from the dead: "Receive the Holy Spirit. If you forgive the sins of any they are forgiven them" (John 20:22-23). Jesus has given his power to forgive sins to the priests of his Church. As a priest I can say that nothing gives me greater joy than to celebrate the sacrament of forgiveness, the sacrament of reconciliation, with a fellow sinner and to say "I absolve you from all your sins in the name of the Father, and of the Son and of the Holy Spirit". As St Paul says:

> All this is from God, who reconciled us to himself through Christ, and has given us the ministry of reconciliation; that is, in Christ God was reconciling the world to himself, not counting their trespasses against them, and entrusting the message of reconciliation to us.
>
> 2 Corinthians 5:18-19

Christ is our peace

We can sum up the whole Gospel message of our salvation with those four words: *Christ is our peace*. The human heart yearns for peace. People who have everything that this world can provide but lack peace of heart are very unhappy. The big bank account, the big job or the big car cannot fill the heart with peace. Only love fills the heart. The three first fruits of the Spirit are "love, joy and peace" (Galatians 5:22). These are spiritual gifts. They are given to the heart that is open to God. The heart that is closed to God is closed to the spiritual world and cannot receive the spiritual fruits of love, joy and peace. Why are so many people in our world unhappy? So often they are looking for happiness in all the wrong places. St John Paul II gives us the secret of happiness in this succinct phrase: "Happiness is being rooted in love".[109] Jesus' whole message is about love: about God's love for us in creating us, about Christ's love for

---

109 *Man and Woman He Created Them*, 16:2.

us in redeeming us, and about the love we should have in our hearts for our neighbours whom we love as we love ourselves. Indeed, as Jesus says we have love in our hearts even for our enemies (Matthew 5:44). Sin is a failure to love. Sin uses others or abuses others; sin always puts selfish self-satisfaction before everything else.

The Second Vatican Council gives us the reason why selfishness, sin, never yields peace:

> If human beings are the only creatures on earth that God has wanted for their own sake, they can fully discover their true selves only in sincere self-giving.[110]

Selfishness or self-seeking is the opposite of self-giving. People who never make that sincere gift of self to anyone, who never truly love, lock themselves within their false self and remain unfulfilled and unhappy. They never discover their true self. Self-giving is a good description of what we mean by love. As we saw in chapter 3, St John Paul II formulated this helpful principle to develop the teaching of the council:

> We have *"the power to express love: precisely that love in which the human person becomes a gift and –* through this gift *–* fulfils the very meaning of his or her being and existence".[111]

Self-giving is, of course, your best gift to the person you love, but notice the great good it brings to yourself: "through this gift you fulfil the very meaning of your being and existence". That is why happiness is rooted in love. Pope Francis continues John Paul's teaching with these words:

> We discover a profound law of reality: that life is attained and matures in the measure that it is offered up in order to give life to others. This is certainly what mission means.[112]

---

110 *Gaudium et Spes*, 24.
111 *Man and Woman He Created Them*, 15:1.
112 *Evangelii Gaudium*, 10.

People who never experienced the joy of this self-giving love will find it hard to accept what Pope Francis is saying. The truth is really only fully understood when it is experienced in action.

Sin is the big lie about what yields happiness. Sin, while it promises happiness, yields the opposite. We quickly discover that instead of bringing happiness, sin causes sadness, distress, division, isolation and ultimately can leave a person friendless. As people begin to discover the good news of our salvation, the kerygma, they begin to realise that living the Gospel is the only way to experience true happiness in this world. As St Paul says, "There is more happiness in giving than in receiving" (Acts 20:35).

Self-giving, and not "acute self-centredness" and self-seeking, is the royal road to happiness. We are all invited by God to walk that royal road. Sin is the one roadblock that can obstruct our walk. But we have good news even about our sins. All our sins will be forgiven when we turn to Christ and our hearts will be filled once again with that true love that brings us peace. Christ is our peace.

Our secularised society

Many people today have no concept of what we mean by the spiritual world. We live in a very secularised society where God may never get a mention. We often hear it said that we are living in a "post-truth" age, the age of relativism, where what is true for you is not true for me. There is no such thing as "the truth". Pope Benedict XVI said that we live in a society plagued by "the tyranny of relativism". "Keep your own truth to yourself and don't try to push it down other's throats" seems to be a strategy for not having to face up to the big moral, social or even spiritual challenges of our times. But even those who hold this very relativistic view of life can easily understand what we mean when we speak about peace of heart. They have searched everywhere for it. If they notice that peace within you, they may ask how one gets this peace of heart. This can be the moment that St Peter had in mind when he wrote: "Always be ready to make your defence to anyone who demands from you an account of the hope that is in you; yet do it with gentleness and reverence" (1 Peter 3:15-16). You can simply say that because you believe in God, you have discovered that Christ is our peace. Because they have asked you, you can tell them that if they open their hearts to what they believe to be truly good and wholesome, and especially if they open their hearts to Jesus Christ, they will begin to experience peace. You could even suggest that they begin to make this affirmation: "I desire peace for my heart and I am willing to give up everything that robs my heart of true peace." That would be a very good prayer for someone who says he doesn't believe in God. You could also gently say, "Christ is our peace, my peace, and whenever I lose my peace I ask Christ to forgive my sins and he restores my peace." You have now sown a seed of the Gospel. If it falls into a heart that is honestly and sincerely seeking true peace, it will take root and grow and in God's time produce a harvest of conversion and new life in that person.

Peace of heart is a pure gift that only Christ can give us; it is the gift of his salvation. He says to us, "Peace I leave with you, my peace I give to you. I do not give to you as the world gives. Do not let your hearts be troubled, and do not let them be afraid" (John 14:27). That is why our message of salvation is called "the good news".

The good news proclaims what Christ is doing now

News is what is happening in the present; history is what happened in the past. The Gospel is the good news of what God is doing in the present, doing for us and the whole human race through the risen Christ who is present in our world, present in his Church, present in you as you speak about him to others and present in those to whom you are speaking. The risen Jesus was present in his missionary disciples in the ancient Roman Empire that was full of temples to pagan gods, and he is present in his disciples in our secularised world that would be happy to banish all symbols of religious faith. We never lose heart for the conversion of our secularised world, just as our ancestors in the faith never lost heart for the conversion of the pagan Roman Empire. Our hope for the new evangelisation is not in our own persuasive abilities but in the faithfulness of Christ.

The great commission

The risen Christ commissioned his disciples to preach the Gospel of salvation to the ends of the earth. His death and resurrection will be the heart of their proclamation. St Luke, in his account of the resurrection appearances of Christ to his disciples, wrote:

> Then he opened their minds to understand the scriptures, and he said to them, "Thus it is written that the Messiah is to suffer and to rise from the dead on the third day, and that repentance and forgiveness of sins is to be proclaimed in his name to all nations, beginning from Jerusalem. You are witnesses of these things."
>
> Luke 24:45-48

St Matthew records the risen Jesus' commissioning of the disciples with these words:

> All authority in heaven and on earth has been given to me. Go therefore and make disciples of all nations, baptising them in the name of the Father and of the Son and of the Holy Spirit, and teaching them to obey everything that I have commanded you. And remember, I am with you always, to the end of the age.
>
> Matthew 28:18-20

Missionary disciples have always taken new heart in that great promise of the Lord, namely, "I am with you always".

St Mark records Christ's commissioning of his disciples with these words:

> Go into all the world and proclaim the good news to the whole creation... So then the Lord Jesus, after he had

141

> spoken to them, was taken up into heaven and sat down at the right hand of God. And they went out and proclaimed the good news everywhere, while the Lord worked with them and confirmed the message by the signs that accompanied it.
>
> Mark 16:15. 19-20

St Mark highlights the fact that Jesus is working with the disciples as they preach the Gospel. He has been working with his disciples during the past two thousand years as they brought the good news of Christ to the "the whole creation". We believe that he is working with us today. As you and the other missionary disciples of your parish confidently engage in the work of the new evangelisation, Christ will be working with you, leading you and guiding you with his Holy Spirit. Jesus says to you, "The harvest is plentiful, but the labourers are few; therefore ask the Lord of the harvest to send out labourers into his harvest" (Luke 10:2). Perhaps that is the first prayer to say when you gather to discuss the urgent need for the new evangelisation in your parish?

Personal spiritual exercise for internalising the message of this chapter

- Find a quiet place as free of interruptions and disruptions as possible. Centre yourself; sitting upright; breathing rhythmically; clearing your mind of all preoccupations.

- As you cross the threshold of stillness, you have come into God's presence.

- In your heart entrust yourself, with all your joys and troubles, with all your good works and sinful weaknesses to Christ our Saviour.

- Thank Jesus for all that he has done for you: his death on the cross, his, resurrection from the dead and the sending of the Holy Spirit.

- Acknowledge him as your Saviour with the words of acclamation after the consecration at Mass, "Save us, Saviour of the world for by your cross and resurrection you have set us free."

- Now relax in his presence and listen to what he says to you.

- Focus again on your breathing as you relax in God's presence.

- Now bring yourself gently back to continue your daily routine.

This spiritual exercise, relaxing in God's presence, will help you to personalise the truth that the Gospel is the good news, the kerygma, of Christ's death and resurrection for us.

— Chapter 7 —

The Mass: sacramental celebration of the kerygma

Jesus Christ not only commissioned his disciples to proclaim the kerygma, the good news of our salvation through his death and resurrection, but he also instructed them to do what he did on the night of his Last Supper when he took bread, blessed and broke it and gave to them saying "this is my body given for you". And, when he took the cup and said "this cup is the new covenant in my blood which will be poured out for you. Do this in remembrance of me". Ever since then the Catholic Church has done that because the sacrament of the Body and Blood of Christ is the source of the whole life of the Church. St John Paul II emphasised this very strongly in his last encyclical letter:

> The Church draws her life from the Eucharist. This truth does not simply express a daily experience of faith, but recapitulates *the heart of the mystery of the Church*. In a variety of ways she joyfully experiences the constant fulfilment of the promise: "Lo, I am with you always, to the close of the age" (Matthew 28:20), but in the Holy Eucharist, through the changing of bread and wine into the Body and Blood of the Lord, she rejoices in this presence with unique intensity. Ever since Pentecost, when the Church, the People of the New Covenant, began her pilgrim journey towards her heavenly homeland, the Divine Sacrament has continued to mark the passing of her days, filling them with confident hope.[113]

We know that the first community of Christians in Jerusalem, after they experienced the outpouring of the Holy Spirit at Pentecost,

---

113 St John Paul II, *Ecclesia in Eucharistia* ("On the Eucharist in its Relationship to the Church"), 1.

began the great work of evangelisation fortified by prayer and the celebration of the Mass. We read this report in Acts:

> They devoted themselves to the apostles' teaching and fellowship, to the breaking of bread and the prayers... Day by day, as they spent much time together in the temple, they broke bread at home.
>
> Acts 2:42. 46

Those first Christians, because they had no churches, celebrated Mass in their own homes. The Mass was called "the breaking of the bread".

The very first description of the celebration of the Eucharist is found in a letter by St Paul. Writing to the Corinthians probably in AD 57, twenty-four years after the death and resurrection of Jesus, Paul said:

> For I received from the Lord what I also handed on to you, that the Lord Jesus on the night when he was betrayed took a loaf of bread, and after he had given thanks, he broke it and said, "This is my body that is for you. Do this in remembrance of me." In the same way he took the cup also, after supper, saying, "This cup is the new covenant in my blood. Do this, as often as you drink it, in remembrance of me." For as often as you eat this bread and drink the cup, *you proclaim the Lord's death until he comes.*
>
> 1 Corinthians 11:23-26
> NB: italics are my own addition

Notice that it was from the risen Jesus who appeared to him in a blinding light on the road to Damascus that Paul received the revelation of the mystery of the Mass. His letter to the Corinthians lets us see how the first Christian generation understood this central event of their Sunday worship: they were proclaiming the death of the Lord until he comes. The disciples were sent forth to proclaim the death and resurrection of Jesus in their preaching, in the kerygma form that we discussed in the last chapter, but they were also told by the Lord to celebrate his death and resurrection in the sacramental form, in the celebration of the Eucharist.

Our Mass, then, is not just devotion. It is the kerygma incarnate, the proclamation of the death and resurrection of Jesus who becomes present on the altar under the appearance of bread and wine. It is the risen Jesus who is present. Let us remind ourselves how the celebration of the Mass proclaims the death and resurrection of the Lord. We find the answer to this question in the Gospel story of the Last Supper. Listen to St Luke's account:

> When the hour came, he took his place at the table, and the apostles with him. He said to them, "I have eagerly desired to eat this Passover with you before I suffer; for I tell you, I will not eat it until it is fulfilled in the kingdom of God"... Then he took a loaf of bread, and when he had given thanks, he broke it and gave it to them, saying, "This is my body, which is given for you. Do this in remembrance of me." And he did the same with the cup after supper, saying, "This cup that is poured out for you is the new covenant in my blood."
>
> Luke 22:14-16. 19-20

This Passover meal was the most solemn Jewish liturgy of the whole year. It was the feast when the Jews recalled with thanksgiving how God had liberated them from slavery in Egypt. Jesus said he "eagerly desired" to share this Passover meal with them before he suffered because during this Passover meal a new liberation would take place; a new covenant would be proclaimed; and he would give them his very body and blood, under the appearance of bread and wine as a perpetual reminder of his death and resurrection.

Jesus' promise

Sometime before Jesus shared his Last Supper with his apostles he had given one of his great teachings in the synagogue in Capernaum, his local synagogue[114] in which he declared, "I am the living bread that came down from heaven. Whoever eats of this bread will live for ever; and the bread that I will give for the life of the world is my flesh" (John 6:51). There were strong objections to what Jesus had said but he continued, with still greater emphasis:

> Very truly, I tell you, unless you eat the flesh of the Son of Man and drink his blood, you have no life in you. Those who eat my flesh and drink my blood have eternal life, and I will raise them up on the last day; for my flesh is true food and my blood is true drink. Those who eat my flesh and drink my blood abide in me, and I in them.
>
> John 6:53-56

When they heard this amazing proclamation of Jesus many of his disciples walked away saying, "This teaching is difficult; who can accept it?" (John 6:60). Jesus didn't try to stop them leaving him. He didn't say, "I am just speaking symbolically" or "This is just a parable." Jesus went to great lengths to explain his parables to his disciples (see Matthew 13). Although Jesus knew that many of his disciples were shocked and dismayed at his proclamation that his flesh was "true food" and his blood was "true drink" he was not going to water it down. He meant what he said. In fact, he was quite prepared to let the Twelve Apostles go if they were not willing to accept his teaching. He turned to them and said, "What about you, do you want to go away too?" Jesus is making it very clear that any disciple who is not prepared to accept what he has just said about the need to eat his flesh and drink his blood should depart. His whole mission hinges on what he said about being "the living bread which came down from heaven" (John 6:51), about what we call the Eucharist. Simon Peter answered, "Lord, to whom shall we go? You have the words of eternal life. We have come to believe and know that you are the Holy One of God" (John 6:67-69). Peter was the one who responded to Jesus when he asked the disciples, "But who do

---

114 Although Jesus grew up in Nazareth and was called the Nazarene, he moved to Capernaum when he began his public ministry. See Matthew 4:13.

you say that I am?" with the words "You are the Messiah, the Son of the living God" (Matthew 16:16). Now in this new situation, when many of the disciples are deserting Jesus, Peter speaks up again and says "you have the message of eternal life". Peter, the spokesman for the Twelve, is prepared to accept that Jesus has given them the "words of eternal life" and so he says "we believe". He didn't say we understand, we know how you are going to fulfil this promise. He knew that what Jesus said could only be accepted in the faith that "Jesus is the Holy One of God".

Those disillusioned disciples who walked away were not present at the Last Supper when Jesus gave his apostles (and us) his Body and Blood as the sacrament of the new covenant. He is giving them his Body and Blood to eat and drink, not in the physical, un-resurrected state, but in the resurrected state, the sacramental state, brought about by his death and resurrection through the power of the Holy Spirit. Just as the Son of God became the Son of Mary by the power of the Holy Spirit, so our gifts of bread and wine offered by the priest at the altar become the Body and Blood of the resurrected and glorified Lord Jesus through that same Spirit. Over our gifts of bread and wine the priest imposes his hands and prays:

> Therefore, O Lord, we humbly implore you: by the same spirit graciously make holy these gifts we have brought to you for consecration that they may become the Body and Blood of your Son our Lord Jesus Christ, at whose command we celebrate these mysteries.

The Mass is not just a remembrance of a past event, the Last Supper, it is the sacramental presence of Christ's redemptive death and resurrection. We were not physically present on calvary when Christ died for us but when we gather to celebrate the Mass, the hour of our salvation becomes sacramentally present to us. St John Paul II said:

When the Church celebrates the Eucharist, the memorial of her Lord's death and resurrection, this central event of salvation becomes really present and "the work of our redemption is carried out". This sacrifice is so decisive for the salvation of the human race that Jesus Christ offered it and returned to the Father only *after he had left us a means of sharing in it* as if we had been present there.[115]

What a wonderful insight John Paul gives us when he says Jesus didn't return to the Father until he had left us the opportunity of sharing in his great sacrifice for our salvation "as if we had been present there"! That is what is happening when we celebrate the Mass. The very moment of our redemption becomes sacramentally resent to us on the altar. Christ's eternal offering of himself for our salvation becomes present in our time. We are at the same Mass as the apostles were at when they celebrated the Last Supper with Jesus. As St Paul said "we are proclaiming the death of the Lord until he comes". We are at no disadvantage because we were not present at the table in the upper room in Jerusalem on that first Holy Thursday evening when Jesus gave us the gift of his Body and Blood in the Eucharist. Each time we gather to celebrate the Mass we are present at the same sacrifice of his Body and Blood under the appearance of the bread and wine. At each Mass Jesus says to us, "take and eat, this is my Body" and "take and drink for this is my Blood of the new and eternal covenant". Because Christ's redemptive sacrifice is so essential for our salvation we had to have some tangible and visible way of being close to it, of feeling that it is happening for us in the present. That is why Jesus, knowing our human weakness, left us the Eucharist, the sacrament of his Body and Blood, so that we could share in it, just as the apostles shared in it on that first Holy Thursday evening, just as Christians throughout the past two thousand years share in it every time they celebrated the Eucharist.

---

115 *Ecclesia de Eucharistia*, 11.

Each time we go to Mass we are proclaiming the death and resurrection of the Lord. We are seated with Jesus at the table as he says to us, "take and eat, this is my Body and take and drink this is my Blood". We receive sacramentally the same Body and Blood of the risen Lord that the Twelve Apostles received at that first Mass. As St John Paul II said:

> In this gift of the Eucharist Jesus Christ entrusted to the Church the perennial making present of the paschal mystery.[116]

Paschal mystery

The paschal mystery is the great sign of God's love for us as Jesus offered himself on the cross for our salvation. The word "paschal" needs a few words of explanation. It has its origin in the Jewish feast of Passover (*pesach* in Hebrew) which commemorates the deliverance of God's people from slavery in Egypt. The angel of God passed over the Israelite homes that had their lintels and doorposts marked with the blood of a lamb slain for the occasion (Exodus 12:21-24). Ever since then the Jews have celebrated their Passover and share a "paschal meal" by eating "the paschal lamb". The paschal lamb, symbol of their deliverance from Egypt, prefigured the Lord Jesus whom St John the Baptist called "the lamb of God who takes away the sin of the world" (John 1:29). It was while Jesus was gathered with the apostles to eat the Passover meal that he gave this solemn religious commemoration, sacred to God's people of the old covenant, a whole new meaning. He declared that God is now ratifying the new covenant that he had promised to give to his people:

> The days are surely coming, says the Lord, when I will make new covenant with the house of Israel and the house of Judah. It will not be like the covenant I made with their ancestors when I took them by the hand to bring them out of the land of Egypt – a covenant that they broke, though I

---

116 *Ecclesia de Eucharistia*, 5.

was their husband, says the Lord. But this is the covenant that I will make with the house of Israel after those days, says the Lord: I will put my law within them, and I will write it on their hearts; and I will be their God, and they shall be my people.

Jeremiah 31:31-33

Christians have believed that at his Last Supper with his apostles, at that special Passover meal, we had the transition from the old covenant to the new covenant. The Lord's Supper, the Eucharist, is the meal that celebrates and remembers how God entered into his new covenant with us. Jesus proclaimed: "This cup that is poured out for you is the new covenant in my blood" (Luke 22:20). The Mass is our celebration of the new covenant, of the paschal mystery, of our redemption from sin, through the passion, death, resurrection and ascension into heaven of our saviour Jesus Christ. As Pope Benedict XVI wrote:

> The institution of the Eucharist demonstrates how Jesus' death, for all its violence and absurdity, became in him a supreme act of love and mankind's definitive deliverance from evil.[117]

The sacrifice of Christ

The Mass makes sacramentally present to us, under the appearance of bread and wine, what is preached in the kerygma, the paschal mystery, and the redeeming sacrifice that Christ offered to the Father on our behalf. That is why St Paul says, "For as often as you eat this bread and drink the cup, you proclaim the Lord's death until he comes" (1 Corinthians 11:26). The celebration of the Mass is the great proclamation of our salvation. It is the great kerygmatic event in the life of the Church, in the life of your parish. You are involved in this great kerygmatic event of the Mass. You are proclaiming Christ's death and resurrection. Even if you never mount the pulpit

---

117 *Sacramentum Caritatis*, 10.

to preach or go out to a public meeting to share your faith, your very participation in the mystery of the Mass is a proclamation of the death and resurrection of Jesus Christ.

Jesus is the high priest at each Mass and what he does is the mystery. It is he who sends forth his Spirit on the bread and wine and transforms them into his very Body and Blood on the altar. Yet how do we proclaim Christ's death and resurrection in the celebration of the Eucharist? I will focus just on two actions that we take, we listen to God's word and we offer ourselves to God.[118]

Listening at the table of God's word

The first thing we do at Mass is we take our place at the table of God's word and listen to what God has to say to us. The Second Vatican Council, which introduced this image of "the table of the Word," said:

> In the sacred books the Father who is in heaven comes lovingly to meet his children and talks with them. And such is the force and the power of the word of God that it can serve the Church as her support and vigour, and the children of the Church as strength for their faith, food for their soul, and a pure and lasting fount of spiritual life.[119]

God speaks to us as the scripture is being proclaimed. We have to listen reverently and intently. If we are not nourished at the table of the word of God it will be very difficult for us to find our true nourishment at the other table set before us in the Mass, the table of the Body of the Lord. Listening to the word of God that is proclaimed in the first part of the Mass is called "the liturgy of the Word". Fr James Mallon gives us this necessary reminder:

---

118 For a fuller explanation of how we are involved in the celebration of the mystery of the Mass, see my book, *Going to Mass: becoming the Eucharist we celebrate* (Chawton: Redemptorist Publications, 2015).

119 Second Vatican Council, *Dei Verbum* ("Constitution on Divine Revelation"), 21.

The word "liturgy" comes from the Greek *leitourgia*, and means "the work of the people". Coming to the liturgy means showing up for work.[120]

Listening to the word of God proclaimed can be hard work. But it is not an optional exercise. If we really desire to enter deeply into the mystery of the Mass and "proclaim the death of the Lord until he comes again", we have to give our full and undivided attention to Christ who speaks to us. We listen in faith to what God is saying because without hearing his word we will not be able to enter into the mystery of the Mass. Pope Benedict said:

> Word and Eucharist are so deeply bound together that we cannot understand one without the other.[121]

Without the action of the Holy Spirit the bread and wine that we offer at Mass cannot be changed into the Body and Blood of Christ. And without that same action of the Holy Spirit in our hearts we cannot hear and receive the word of God. It is very helpful, therefore, to invoke the Holy Spirit to enlighten us as the holy scripture is being proclaimed. As Alexander Schmemann, the great Greek Orthodox theologian wrote:

> Like the consecration of the gifts, understanding and acceptance of the word depend not on us, not only on our desires, but above all on the sacramental transformation of the "eyes of our mind", on the coming of the Holy Spirit.[122]

Without that light of the Holy Spirit we will not be able to hear what God is saying to us in the Mass.

Listening in faith

St Jerome said, "We cannot come to an understanding of Scripture without the assistance of the Holy Spirit who inspired it".[123] As we

---

120 Mallon, *Divine Renovation*, 121.
121 Pope Benedict XVI, *Verbum Domini* ("Post-Synodal Exhortation on the Word of God"), 55.
122 Alexander Schmemann, *The Eucharist: sacrament of the kingdom* (New York: St Vladimir's Seminary Press, 2000), 76.
123 *Verbum Domini*, 16.

allow the Holy Spirit to open our hearts we will begin to hear the words of scripture in a new way. St Paul tells us that "the word of God is living and active" (Hebrews 4:12). It is not a word from the past, about some situation in the past. It is spoken to us in the present. But without faith we will not be able to hear it as a personal word. St Thomas Aquinas said:

> The letter even of the Gospel would kill were there not the inward grace of healing faith.[124]

Without faith in Christ's presence in the Blessed Sacrament we cannot receive Holy Communion. Likewise, without faith we will not be able to hear the word of God as the scriptures are being proclaimed. Invoking the Holy Spirit to enlighten our minds as we listen to the scripture being proclaimed is the necessary preparation for hearing the word of God. And, once we hear the word of God we will be ready to proclaim it. Once we hear the word of God in the Mass our hearts are ready to "proclaim the death of the Lord until he comes again", we are ready to proclaim the kerygma.

We offer ourselves to God at Mass

The first action we perform when we sit at the table of the word of God during Mass is to listen to God who is speaking to us. It is by God's word that we want to live. Jesus said to us, "One does not live by bread alone but by every word that comes from the mouth of God" (Matthew 4:4). The second action is equally important. We bring our gifts to the altar, simple gifts of bread and wine, we present them to the priest and then, on our behalf, the priest offers them to God. As the General Instruction on the Roman Missal says:

> In the celebration of Mass the faithful form a holy people, a people of God's own possession and a royal priesthood, so that they may give thanks to God and offer the unblemished

---

124 St Thomas Aquinas, *Summa Theologica*, 1a-IIae, question 106, part 2.

> sacrificial victim not only by means of the hands of the Priest but also together with him and so that they may learn to offer their very selves.[125]

Notice those two fundamental offerings that we all make at Mass: we offer the "the unblemished sacrificial victim" with the priest, and we offer ourselves to God. We assemble for Mass to make this twofold offering not as a group of isolated individuals but as Church, as the Body of Christ, to *celebrate* the Mass, and not just *to be present at* the Mass. The congregations assemble to celebrate the Mass which is the action of the whole assembly. As the General Instruction emphasises:

> The faithful are to form one body, whether in hearing the Word of God, or by taking part in the prayers and in the singing, or above all by the common offering of the Sacrifice and by participating together at the Lord's table.[126]

It is not just the priest who is offering the gifts. The whole congregation offers the bread and wine with the priest. And, most importantly of all, we all offer ourselves to God as we do so. The priest cannot make that offering of ourselves for us; we have to do it for ourselves. St Paul said, "Think of God's mercy and worship him, I beg you, in a way that is worthy of thinking beings, by offering your living bodies as a holy sacrifice, truly pleasing to God" (Romans. 12:1). On St Paul's exhortation to make this offering of our bodies, Pope Benedict XVI commented:

> In these words the new worship appears as a total self-offering made in communion with the whole Church. The apostle's insistence on the offering of our bodies emphasizes the concrete human reality of a worship which is anything but disincarnate.[127]

---

125 The General Introduction of the Roman Missal, 95.
126 The General Introduction of the Roman Missal, 96.
127 Pope Benedict XVI, *Heart of the Christian Life* (San Francisco: Ignatius Press, 2010), 75.

The symbolic meaning of a gift

How do we offer ourselves to God? We do it symbolically. Our gifts of bread and wine, which are offered at the altar, represent ourselves. This is a most important moment in our celebration of the Mass. Gift-giving is one of the most beautiful human actions we can engage in. We all like to receive gifts for special times in our lives like birthdays or weddings or anniversaries. And we all like to give gifts. There is nothing more innate in the human heart than the urge to give a gift. But what are we trying to say when we give a friend or loved one a gift? Suppose it is your birthday and your best friend wants to give you a gift. He or she knows what you like. So your friend presents you with a beautiful bottle of wine. What is going on in that gift-giving? Is your friend saying, "It's your birthday, you love wine," or, is your friend saying, "It's your birthday, I love you." If the gift is not saying "I love you" it is not a gift at all. It is an investment! Your friend will be having a birthday before too long!

Notice that there is a new dynamic created in the very act of gift-giving. Your friend is the *giver* of the gift to you and you become the *thanksgiver* to your friend for the beautiful gift, the symbol of love. You recognise in the gift a new expression of your friend's love. Indeed, in receiving the gift you are receiving the love of your friend; your friend's very self. And, as you gratefully receive the gift, your love is renewed and strengthened. That manifestation of true love brings peace and joy, healing and reconciliation. The same dynamic is at work when we give God our gift. We are the *giver* of the gift and God becomes *thanksgiver* to us for our gift. We are making a great proclamation as our gifts of bread and wine are offered to God. We are saying, as a congregation gathered for the Mass, "God our Father, we love you." The bread and wine that we offer to God are received gratefully by the Father because it is the symbol of our love for him, the sign that we are now making a gift of ourselves to him in love and thanksgiving. The bread and wine represent "all that is within me" (Psalm 103:1); all the good and all the bad; all the light and all the darkness; all the virtue and all the vice; our whole being.

The Offertory of the Mass can be a time of deep inner healing: our hurts and our inner wounds; our disappointment and our frustrations; our family upsets and our struggles with colleagues at work; our grief at the death of a loved one or the pain of a marriage break-up, all these fabrics of our lives we offer to God. At this stage of bringing our gifts to the altar it is important for us not to exclude any part of our lives, no matter how sinful something may have been. We have to offer to God everything about us. The Father knows everything and he invites us to lovingly and trustingly offer him everything.

The Consecration

Those two actions of listening to God's word and offering ourselves to God prepare our minds and hearts to be open to the mystery of faith, to what God is doing in the celebration of the Mass. During the great prayer of Consecration we implore God to take our gifts of bread and wine, that he has received, and through the Holy Spirit transform them into the very Body and Blood of Jesus Christ our Saviour. We have a variety of prayers of Consecration. Consider just this one:

> Look, we pray, upon your people's offerings and pour out on them the power of your Spirit, that they may become the Body and Blood of your beloved Son, Jesus Christ, in whom we, too, are your sons and daughters.[128]

The great miracle of our faith happens. Christ becomes truly present on the altar under the appearance of bread and wine. The whole congregation acknowledges this as they are invited to "proclaim the mystery of faith". We respond with the acclamation: "We proclaim your death, O Lord, and profess your resurrection until you come again." This response shows us that we are seeing the Mass today in the same way that St Paul saw it two thousand years ago: "For as often as you eat this bread, and drink the cup, you proclaim the Lord's death until he comes" (1 Corinthians 11:26). In the Mass

---

128 Mass for Reconciliation, 1.

we are making that great proclamation to one another. This is what we believe. The risen Christ is in our midst. As St John Paul II reminded us:

> The Eucharistic sacrifice makes present not only the mystery of the Saviour's passion and death, but also the mystery of the resurrection which crowned his sacrifice.[129]

During Mass we proclaim the kerygma to one another. The Mass is the liturgical proclamation of the Eucharistic presence of the risen Christ on the altar. Immediately after the Consecration when the bread and wine become the Body and Blood of Christ, the priest invokes the Holy Spirit again to come on all present with the words, "Grant that we who are nourished by the Body and Blood of your Son and filled with his Holy Spirit may become one body, one spirit in Christ".[130] That is a big request that only God can bring about. We are asking to be so united in Christ that we will be just one body, one Spirit. As St Paul says so often in his letters "We, who are many, are one body in Christ" (Romans 12:5; see also 1 Corinthians 12:27 and Ephesians 1:23).

Holy Communion

The mystery of faith, then, is twofold. The bread and wine are changed into the Body and Blood of Christ and we too are transformed and become "one body, one Spirit in Christ". The Body of Christ becomes truly present under the appearance of the bread and wine on the altar and, at the same time, the Body of Christ becomes mystically present in the disciples around the altar. That is the profound mystery of our faith involving both Christ and us. The new *Catechism of the Catholic Church* teaches the depth of the mystery of our faith by quoting the words of St Augustine:

> If you are the body and members of Christ, then it is your sacrament that is placed on the table of the Lord; it is your

---

129 *Ecclesia de Eucharistia*, 15.
130 Third Eucharistic Prayer.

sacrament that you receive. To that which you respond, "Amen" ("yes, it is true") and by responding to it you ascent to it. For you hear the word, "the Body of Christ" and respond "Amen". Be then a member of the Body of Christ so that your Amen may be true.[131]

The Mass is the mystery not just of Christ becoming truly present in our gift of bread and wine but also of Christ becoming mystically present in all of us sharing in the mystery of the Mass. The ultimate reason why Christ becomes truly present on the altar is because he yearns to be truly present in us, to make us "sharers in his divinity", to live his eternal life in and through us. As he said, "He who eats my flesh and drinks my blood lives in me and I live in him" (John 6:56). St Augustine was very aware that the mystery of us becoming the Body of Christ can be too easily overlooked. All our focus tends to be on Christ truly present under the appearance of bread and wine on the altar. It is easier, less challenging, to adore Christ at a distance, to keep him, as it were, on the altar. That can fill us with great devotion and reverence. It is much more challenging, however, to see Christ present in those who have gathered for the Mass, in "the sacred assembly" of the faithful, or to see him present in those who are poor, homeless or marginalised on the streets outside the church. That can make great demands on our generosity towards certain people and challenge us to let go of bad attitudes. St John Chrysostom, the great Patriarch of Constantinople (present-day Istanbul) said:

> You have tasted the Blood of the Lord, yet you do not recognise your brother... You dishonour this table when you do not judge worthy of sharing your food with someone judged worthy to take part in this meal. God freed you from all your sins and invited you here, but you have not become more merciful.[132]

---

131 *Catechism of the Catholic Church*, 1396.
132 *Catechism of the Catholic Church*, 1397.

Becoming the Eucharist we celebrate

St John Chrysostom is saying that it is possible to come to the Eucharist without doing what Jesus did. When Jesus asked us to "do this in memory of me" what exactly was the "this" that he was referring to? Was he saying "just repeat the ritual that I have performed with the bread and wine" or was he saying "do the full meaning of what I have just done"? We find the same verbs used in all the accounts of what Jesus did at the Last Supper to bring out the full meaning of what he was doing: he took the bread, he blessed the bread, he broke the bread, and he shared the broken bread that had become his body with his disciples. That action of breaking the bread was so significant in the early Christian community, that the name given to the celebration of the Eucharist was "the breaking of the bread". We too break the consecrated bread at Mass, but we can easily forget that before the bread and wine became the Body and Blood of Christ on the altar they were the gifts that we offered to God, gifts symbolising the gift that we were making of ourselves to God. Now in "the breaking of the bread" it is ourselves, so often closed in on ourselves that we have to break open and be willing to share as members of Christ. Fr Cantalamessa recounts how he began to see the Eucharist with new eyes when he realised, that to do what Jesus did meant that he too had to "break" everythin within himself that was not totally given to God and God's people.

> Then I understood that to "do" what Jesus did that night, I must, first of all, "break" myself and that is, lay before God all hardness, all rebellion towards him or towards others, crush my pride, submit and say "yes", fully, to all that God asks of me. I too must repeat the words, Lo, I have come to do thy will, O God! You don't want many things from me; you want me and I say "yes". To be Eucharist like Jesus signifies being totally abandoned to the Father's will.[133]

---

133 Raniero Cantalamessa, *The Eucharist* (Collegeville: Liturgical Press, 1995), 18.

To do what Jesus did means that we must become the Eucharist we celebrate. We must repent of any spirit of selfishness, meanness, arrogance, fault-finding and condemning of others. Then we can truly offer to others our service of love and acceptance, especially to those who are poor or rejected in our society. As Pope Benedict XVI said:

> The Eucharist, since it embraces the concrete, everyday existence of the believer, makes possible, day by day, the progressive transfiguration of all those called by grace to reflect the image of the Son of God.[134]

How can we grow in this appreciation of the mystery of the Mass and reverence the Body of Christ, not just on the altar, but in those who are around the altar, and in those who are abandoned on our streets? Am I willing to "break the bread" of my life in a relationship where I haven't been giving my all in love and service? If I have been carrying a negative attitude towards somebody or harbouring unforgiveness or bitterness in my heart, am I willing to change? I will certainly not be able to change through my own strength. I will need the great miracle of redemption to be able to become the Eucharist I celebrate.

To do what Jesus did, to become the Eucharist that we celebrate, to be the Body of Christ, we humbly offer ourselves to the Father during Mass and open our hearts to be transformed by the Holy Spirit into the Body of Christ for our brothers and sisters. That is what Jesus wants to do for us. We pray for this transforming grace in each Mass as we say "through the mystery of this water and wine may we come to share in his divine nature who humbled himself to share in our human nature". Celebrating Mass in this spirit means being willing to become the Eucharist we celebrate.

---

134 *Sacramentum Caritatis*, 71.

Sent forth to announce the Gospel

St John Paul II encourages us with these words:

> Proclaiming the death of the Lord "until he comes" (1 Corinthians 11:26) entails that all who take part in the Eucharist be committed to changing their lives and making them in a certain way completely "Eucharistic". It is the fruit of a transfigured existence and a commitment to transforming the world in accordance with the Gospel which splendidly illustrates the eschatological tension inherent in the celebration of the Eucharist and in the Christ life as a whole: Come, Lord Jesus.[135]

When we have completed the celebration of the Mass we don't forget about proclamation of the Gospel until the next Sunday. We are sent forth with the exhortation: "Go and announce the Gospel of the Lord." We have proclaimed to one another during the Mass the death and resurrection of Jesus Christ. After our gifts of bread and wine were transformed by the power of the Holy Spirit into his body and blood we said, "We proclaim your death, O Lord, and profess your resurrection until you come again." Or we may have used another formula such as, "When we eat this Bread and drink this Cup, we proclaim your Death, O Lord, until you come again." We are proclaiming to one another at Mass the death of the Lord until he comes again. As we saw in the last chapter, that is the kerygma. We are revitalised as we celebrate the Mass and we are sent forth to proclaim to others what we have just celebrated in the Mass, the presence of the risen Lord in our midst.

We never cease to be evangelists, missionary disciples of Jesus. We share in the deepest identity of the Church which is, as we have seen, evangelisation. That is why it is good and necessary to be reminded, at the end of our celebration of Mass, that we are now being sent forth to announce the Gospel of the Lord, to evangelise family and

---

135 *Ecclesia de Eucharistia*, 20.

friends, neighbours and our city in the name of Jesus. Christ has chosen us to do this work. He has given us the gift and the light of faith to believe in him. And he says to us:

> You are the light of the world. A city built on a hill cannot be hidden. No one after lighting a lamp puts it under a bushel basket, but on the lampstand, and it gives light to all in the house. In the same way, let your light shine before others, so that they may see your good works and give glory to your Father in heaven.
>
> Matthew 5:1

Participating deeply and reverently in the celebration of the Mass prepares us to "let the light shine", the light of the kerygma, the death and resurrection of Jesus Christ. I give the final word of this book to Pope Francis, who has inspired much of what I have written. He shares with us his deep desire:

> How I long to find the right words to stir up enthusiasm for a new chapter of evangelization full of fervour, joy, generosity, courage, boundless love and attraction. Yet I realize that no words of encouragement will be enough unless the fire of the Holy Spirit burns in our hearts. A spirit-filled evangelization is one guided by the Holy Spirit, for he is the soul of the Church called to proclaim the Gospel.[136]

---

136 *Evangelii Gaudium*, 261.

Personal spiritual exercise for internalising the message of this chapter

- Find a quiet place as free of interruptions and disruptions as possible. Centre yourself; sitting upright; breathing rhythmically; clearing your mind of all preoccupations.

- As you cross the threshold of stillness, you have come into God's presence.

- In your heart entrust yourself, with all your joys and troubles, with all your good works and all your sinful weaknesses to Christ our Saviour.

- Thank Jesus for the gift of the Holy Mass, in which we celebrate his death and resurrection and receive him as "the living bread come down from heaven" (John 6:51).

- As you ask the Lord for the grace you need to have a deeper reverence for the Sunday Mass, relax and wait in his presence. He wants to give you that grace.

- Now bring yourself gently back to continue your daily routine.

This spiritual exercise, relaxing in God's presence, will help you to personalise the truth that, as St John Paul II said, "The Church draws her life from the Eucharist". You want to draw your life from that same divine source.

CHURCH OF
St JOHN VIANNEY
WANTAGE

Fr Jim McManus C.Ss.R.

Jim McManus was professed as a Redemptorist on 8 September 1957 and celebrated the diamond jubilee of his profession in 2017. He was ordained a priest in 1964 and pursued further studies in Rome. After teaching moral theology for six years in the Redemptorist seminary he established Hawkstone Hall as a sabbatical spiritual renewal centre in 1973. For forty years, through three-month renewal courses, Hawkstone offered the opportunity for deep spiritual renewal to thousands of priests and religious men and women from all over the world. His work there led him to write several books on the healing ministry, on developing a spirituality of true self-esteem and forgiveness, and on cultivating true devotion in one's spiritual life. In 2016, during the Holy Year of Mercy, he was commissioned by Pope Francis as a Missionary of Mercy and instructed to assure everyone that once they turn to God and ask for his mercy, the Church embraces them. He is currently based in the Redemptorist Spirituality Centre in Scotland, in Perth, where his main mission consists of preaching parish missions throughout Britain, directing retreats for priests and religious in different countries, and encouraging the development of the healing ministry in parish life.